HUD Housing Programs for Persons with Disabilities

HUD Housing Programs for Persons with Disabilities

Ervin C. Felker
Editor

Nova Science Publishers, Inc.
New York

LIBRARY OF CONGRESS CATALOGING-IN-PUBLICATION DATA

ISBN: 978-1-60741-113-0

Published by Nova Science Publishers, Inc.; New York

CONTENTS

PREFACE

This book explores the ability of persons with disabilities to live independently in affordable, accessible housing. This became a prominent issue starting in 1999 as the result of a Supreme Court decision, Olmstead v. L.C., in which the court held that institutionalization of persons with mental disabilities in lieu of community-based care may constitute discrimination. Shortly after the Olmstead decision, the President announced the New Freedom Initiative, an effort through multiple federal agencies to ensure full participation in society of persons with disabilities. Thus, this book discusses the Department of Housing and Urban Development (HUD)and a number of its programs that provide housing for persons with disabilities in various ways.

Chapter 1 - The ability of persons with disabilities to live independently in affordable, accessible housing became a prominent issue starting in 1999 as the result of a Supreme Court decision, *Olmstead v. L. C.* The court held that institutionalization of persons with mental disabilities in lieu of community-based care may constitute discrimination. Shortly after the *Olmstead* decision, on February 1, 2001, the President announced the New Freedom Initiative, an effort through multiple federal agencies to ensure full participation in society of persons with disabilities. Part of the New Freedom Initiative was Executive Order 13217, which implemented the *Olmstead* decision by ensuring (among other things) that all people with disabilities, not just those with mental illness, benefit from community-based treatment.

In order to ensure that persons with disabilities may live in community settings rather than in institutions, affordable and accessible housing is necessary. The Department of Housing and Urban Development (HUD) operates a number of programs that provide housing for persons with disabilities in various ways. The Section 811 Supportive Housing for Persons with Disabilities program provides capital grants and project rental assistance to nonprofit developers of housing targeted specifically to persons with disabilities. Prior to creation of Section 811, persons with disabilities lived together with elderly residents (defined by HUD as households with one or more adults age 62 or older) in developments funded through the Section 202 Supportive Housing for the Elderly program. The project-based Section 8 and Public Housing programs give project owners the option of dedicating facilities to elderly residents, residents with disabilities, or both populations together. Both the Section 811 and Section 8 programs set aside housing vouchers for persons with disabilities. And two HUD block grant programs — HOME and the Community Development Block Grant — may be used by states and communities to construct or rehabilitate housing for persons with disabilities.

In addition to these HUD programs, the Low Income Housing Tax Credit (LIHTC), administered by the Internal Revenue Service, may be used by states to target housing to special needs populations, including persons with disabilities. The LIHTC may be used in conjunction with HUD grants, including capital grants through the Section 811 program. The Housing and Economic Recovery Act of 2008 (P.L. 110-289) made it possible for developers of Section 811 housing to qualify for a higher tax credit rate, which could potentially make these mixed financing developments more feasible.

In the 1 10th Congress, the Frank Melville Supportive Housing Investment Act (H.R. 5772), a bill that would make changes to the Section 811 program, was approved by the House on September 17, 2008. Among its changes, the bill would turn over funding of Section 811 vouchers to the Section 8 program and would create a demonstration program for Section 811 rental assistance to be used in conjunction with other funding streams, including the LIHTC and HOME program. A version of the bill was also introduced in the Senate (S. 3593). This report will be updated as events warrant.

Chapter 2 - The Department of Justice ("DOJ") and the Department of Housing and Urban Development ("HUD") are jointly responsible for enforcing the federal Fair Housing Act (the "Act"), which prohibits discrimination in housing on the basis of race, color, religion, sex, national origin, familial status, and disability. One type of disability discrimination prohibited by the Act is a refusal to permit, at the expense of the person with a disability, reasonable modifications of existing premises occupied or to be occupied by such person if such modifications may be necessary to afford such person full enjoyment of the premises. HUD and DOJ frequently respond to complaints alleging that housing providers have violated the Act by refusing reasonable modifications to persons with disabilities. This Statement provides technical assistance regarding the rights and obligations of persons with disabilities and housing providers under the Act relating to reasonable modifications.

This Statement is not intended to provide specific guidance regarding the Act's design and construction requirements for multifamily dwellings built for first occupancy after March 13, 1991. Some of the reasonable modifications discussed in this Statement are features of accessible design that are required for covered multifamily dwellings pursuant to the Act's design and construction requirements. As a result, people involved in the design and construction of multifamily dwellings are advised to consult the Act at 42 U.S.C. § 3604(f)(3)(c), the implementing regulations at 24 C.F.R. § 100.205, the Fair Housing Accessibility Guidelines, and the Fair Housing Act Design Manual. All of these are available on HUD's website at www.hud.gov/offices/fheo/disabilities/index.cfm. Additional technical guidance on the design and construction requirements can also be found on HUD's website and the Fair Housing Accessibility FIRST website at: http://www.fairhousingfirst.org.

In: HUD Housing Programs for Persons … ISBN 978-1-60741-113-0
Editor: Ervin C. Felker, pp. 1-49

Chapter 1

SECTION 811 AND OTHER HUD HOUSING PROGRAMS FOR PERSONS WITH DISABILITIES*

Libby Perl
Analyst in Housing Policy, Domestic Social Policy Division

ABSTRACT

The ability of persons with disabilities to live independently in affordable, accessible housing became a prominent issue starting in 1999 as the result of a Supreme Court decision, *Olmstead v. L. C.* The court held that institutionalization of persons with mental disabilities in lieu of community-based care may constitute discrimination. Shortly after the *Olmstead* decision, on February 1, 2001, the President announced the New Freedom Initiative, an effort through multiple federal agencies to ensure full participation in society of persons with disabilities. Part of the New Freedom Initiative was Executive Order 13217, which implemented the *Olmstead* decision by ensuring (among other things) that all people with disabilities, not just those with mental illness, benefit from community-based treatment.

---

* This is an edited, excerpted and augmented edition of a CRS Report for Congress publication, Order Code RL34728, dated November 3, 2008.

In order to ensure that persons with disabilities may live in community settings rather than in institutions, affordable and accessible housing is necessary. The Department of Housing and Urban Development (HUD) operates a number of programs that provide housing for persons with disabilities in various ways. The Section 811 Supportive Housing for Persons with Disabilities program provides capital grants and project rental assistance to nonprofit developers of housing targeted specifically to persons with disabilities. Prior to creation of Section 811, persons with disabilities lived together with elderly residents (defined by HUD as households with one or more adults age 62 or older) in developments funded through the Section 202 Supportive Housing for the Elderly program. The project-based Section 8 and Public Housing programs give project owners the option of dedicating facilities to elderly residents, residents with disabilities, or both populations together. Both the Section 811 and Section 8 programs set aside housing vouchers for persons with disabilities. And two HUD block grant programs — HOME and the Community Development Block Grant — may be used by states and communities to construct or rehabilitate housing for persons with disabilities.

In addition to these HUD programs, the Low Income Housing Tax Credit (LIHTC), administered by the Internal Revenue Service, may be used by states to target housing to special needs populations, including persons with disabilities. The LIHTC may be used in conjunction with HUD grants, including capital grants through the Section 811 program. The Housing and Economic Recovery Act of 2008 (P.L. 110-289) made it possible for developers of Section 811 housing to qualify for a higher tax credit rate, which could potentially make these mixed financing developments more feasible.

In the 1 10th Congress, the Frank Melville Supportive Housing Investment Act (H.R. 5772), a bill that would make changes to the Section 811 program, was approved by the House on September 17, 2008. Among its changes, the bill would turn over funding of Section 811 vouchers to the Section 8 program and would create a demonstration program for Section 811 rental assistance to be used in conjunction with other funding streams, including the LIHTC and HOME program. A version of the bill was also introduced in the Senate (S. 3593). This report will be updated as events warrant.

INTRODUCTION

Persons with physical disabilities, developmental disabilities, or mental illnesses frequently face difficulty in finding suitable housing, together with supportive services (often referred to as person-directed or consumer-directed services), in which they can live as active members of their community. For those individuals with physical disabilities, it may be difficult to find rental units that are accessible, and some prospective residents with disabilities may face discrimination in their search for housing.[1] Zoning laws may also prevent the construction of homes where persons with disabilities live together.[2] In addition, the affordability of housing and services may be an issue. Individuals with disabilities may have low incomes due to the inability to work, the need for additional education and training to find suitable employment, or employer discrimination.[3] Insufficient income can put the costs of in-home care and supportive services out of reach, and services are not always available in all states through programs such as Medicare and Medicaid.[4] As a result of these limitations, among other causes, persons with disabilities may be institutionalized in nursing homes, psychiatric hospitals, or similar facilities rather than living independently.[5] Those individuals not in such facilities may still live in group homes or small multifamily housing developments dedicated to persons with disabilities instead of on their own.[6]

However, national recognition of the need for appropriate housing for persons with disabilities gained support after the 1999 Supreme Court decision in the case of *Olmstead v. L. C.* In that case, two women who had spent years in a psychiatric hospital argued that their institutionalization constituted discrimination under the Americans with Disabilities Act. The Supreme Court agreed, finding that "[s]tates are required to provide community-based treatment for persons with mental disabilities when the State's treatment professionals determine that such placement is appropriate, and the placement can be reasonably accommodated.. ."[7] Shortly after the ruling in *Olmstead*, on February 1, 2001, President Bush announced the "New Freedom Initiative," an effort through multiple federal agencies, in cooperation with the states, to ensure full participation in society of persons with disabilities. Part of the New Freedom Initiative was an Executive Order implementing the *Olmstead* decision to ensure that all people with disabilities, not just those with mental illnesses, benefit from community-based treatment.[8] However, for many states and communities, it may be difficult to achieve the goal of treatment in a community environment without the availability of accessible and affordable housing.[9]

The federal government makes available funds to finance subsidized rental housing for persons with disabilities primarily through the Department of Housing and Urban Development (HUD). The Section 811 Supportive Housing for Persons with Disabilities program is the only federal program that funds supportive housing exclusively for persons with disabilities. However, the Section 811 program is not the only source of funds to provide housing units for persons with disabilities. Over the years, a number of other HUD programs have been used to fund housing units dedicated to persons with disabilities, and many of those units are still in service. These programs include the Section 202 Supportive Housing for the Elderly program, Public Housing, the project-based Section 8 rental assistance program, and the Section 8 voucher program. In recent years, federal block grant programs — the Community Development Block Grant and HOME Investment Partnerships program — have been a source of funds used by states and local communities to develop and rehabilitate housing for persons with disabilities. Another source of funds is the Low Income Housing Tax Credit, administered by the Internal Revenue Service, through which state governments have the discretion to prioritize housing for persons with disabilities.

This report describes how federal funds are used to develop housing designated for persons with disabilities. It also discusses current issues surrounding housing for persons with disabilities, including mixed financing arrangements, worst case housing needs, persons with disabilities who are homeless, and legislation in the 1 10th Congress.

Housing for Persons with Disabilities and the Fair Housing Act

This report discusses federal programs that provide funds to develop affordable rental housing units specifically for persons with disabilities. Individuals with disabilities may also live in housing that has not been specifically designed for their needs, however. The Fair Housing Act (FHA), enacted as part of the Civil Rights Act of 1968, contains provisions that are meant to ensure that persons with disabilities may obtain accessible rental housing even in facilities not specifically designed for them.

The FHA was created to prevent discrimination in the provision of housing based on "race, color, religion, and national origin."[10] In 1988, the Fair Housing Amendments Act (P.L. 100-430) amended the FHA to prevent discrimination based on "handicap." The Fair Housing Act defines a "handicap" as (1) having a physical or mental impairment that substantially limits one or more major life activities, (2) having a record of such impairment, or (3) being perceived as having such impairment.[11] In addition to prohibiting discrimination against persons based on handicap, the FHA imposes affirmative duties on housing providers.

Under the Fair Housing Amendments Act of 1988, if a landlord fails to follow certain requirements to make housing accessible to persons with disabilities, it is considered discrimination. In the area of new construction, beginning 30 months after implementation of P.L. 100-430 (in 1988), it became unlawful for multifamily housing developers to design and construct housing of four or more units that fails to: (1) have common areas that are accessible and useable by persons with disabilities, (2) have doors wide enough to accommodate wheelchairs, and (3) include units with accessible routes through the unit; bathrooms and kitchens that are wheelchair accessible; electrical outlets, light switches and thermostats that are accessible; bathrooms with reinforcements where grab bars may be installed; and kitchens and baths that may be maneuvered through with a wheelchair.[12]

For units in older facilities, or in units not covered by the FHA, the Fair Housing Amendments Act recognized that modifications to units may be necessary to make them accessible to persons with disabilities. Under the law, it is discriminatory for landlords to refuse to allow tenants to make physical changes to the premises — referred to as "reasonable modifications" — where changes are necessary to afford tenants full enjoyment of the premises.[13] In addition, the law gives tenants the right to ask their landlords for "reasonable accommodations" in the rules, policies, practices, or services that ordinarily apply to tenants living in rental property. It is considered discrimination under the FHA for a landlord to refuse to make a reasonable accommodation where it is necessary to give residents with disabilities an equal opportunity to use and enjoy their dwelling unit.[14] Reasonable modifications and reasonable accommodations are described below.

Reasonable Modifications

While the FHA may require landlords to permit tenants to make reasonable modifications to the rental premises, the statute neither defines the term "reasonable modification," nor the circumstances under which modifications might be required to ensure a tenant's enjoyment of the premises. However, HUD and the Department of Justice (DOJ) have published joint guidance describing reasonable modifications.[15] They may include changes to a rental unit such as widening doorways, installing a ramp or grab bars, or lowering cabinets.[16] The HUD/DOJ guidance requires that there be an identifiable relationship between the tenant's disability and the modification; if there is not, a landlord may refuse to allow the alteration.[17] Landlords are not required to pay for modifications, and, if the modifications would prevent a future tenant's enjoyment of the premises, the landlord may require tenants to restore the unit to its original state when moving out. In order to ensure that this occurs, a landlord may require tenants to deposit funds into an escrow account to pay for restoration.[18] However, landlords cannot require tenants to pay a higher security deposit because of modifications to the property.

While no federal program exists specifically to help tenants with disabilities pay for home modifications, funding may be available at the state or local level. For example, some states make funds available through their Medicaid waiver programs to allow persons with disabilities to make modifications.[19] States may also set up grant or loan programs using state, local, or federal funds to assist with home modifications. Sources of federal funds that could be used for this purpose include the HOME Investment Partnerships block grant and the Community Development Block Grant (these programs are described later in this report).

Reasonable Accommodations

In addition to permitting tenants to make reasonable modifications to their units under the FHA, landlords may be required to make "reasonable accommodations" to ensure that tenants with disabilities may use and enjoy their dwelling. Reasonable accommodations may involve altering or making an exception to rules, policies, practices, or services that would otherwise apply to tenants, but when applied to an individual with a disability may prevent them from maintaining their tenancy or fully enjoying use of the facility.[20] As with reasonable modifications, there must be a relationship between the disability and the requested accommodation. However, unlike reasonable modifications, a tenant may request an accommodation that will involve a cost to the housing provider, although the requested accommodation cannot pose an undue financial or administrative burden, and cannot fundamentally alter the provider's operations.[21] If the requested accommodation is reasonable, tenants cannot be charged an extra fee or be required to make a deposit into an escrow account. Examples of reasonable accommodations include changing the manner of rental payment for a tenant with a mental illness so that he or she need not leave the apartment or allowing assistance animals in a building that does not otherwise allow pets.

Section 811 Supportive Housing for Persons with Disabilities Program

The Section 811 Supportive Housing for Persons with Disabilities program is administered by HUD and funds permanent supportive housing for very low-income persons with disabilities (those with household income at or below 50% of area median income). The program primarily provides capital grants and project rental assistance to nonprofit housing developers. Section 811 capital grants can be used for construction, rehabilitation, or acquisition of buildings to be used as housing for persons with disabilities.[22] Nonprofit developers need not repay the capital grants as long as the housing is available and affordable for at least 40 years to very low- income persons with disabilities. The Section 811 program also distributes tenant- based vouchers — sometimes referred to as "mainstream vouchers" — that can be used by eligible tenants to rent housing in the private market.

Evolution of the Section 811 Program

The Section 811 Supportive Housing for Persons with Disabilities program was created as part of the Cranston-Gonzalez Affordable Housing Act of 1990 (P.L. 101- 62 5). Until enactment of Cranston-Gonzalez, HUD had funded housing units for persons with disabilities largely through the Section 202 Supportive Housing for the Elderly program, created in 1959. Over the years, the individuals with disabilities who were eligible for Section 202 housing expanded from persons with physical disabilities to those with developmental disabilities and eventually to individuals with chronic mental illnesses. Over time, Congress also began to implement a split between housing for elderly residents[23] and those with disabilities, ultimately resulting in creation of the Section 811 program. However, units for persons with disabilities that were created as part of the Section 202 program continue to be financed through that program and governed by its rules, so the history of their development continues to be important.[24]

Section 202 Housing for the Elderly or Handicapped

The Section 202 program was created as part of the Housing Act of 1959 (P.L. 86-372) and provided low-interest loans to non-profit developers to construct multifamily housing for families where one or more person is age 62 or older. Section 202 did not initially provide housing for persons with disabilities. Five years after the creation of the Section 202 program, the Housing Act of 1964 (P.L. 88-560) added non-elderly "handicapped" individuals and families to the definition of "elderly families" under the Section 202 program. At the time, "handicapped" was defined by P.L. 88-560 as a physical impairment (1) expected to be of long-continued or indefinite duration, (2) that substantially impedes the ability to live independently, and (3) is of such a nature that the ability to live independently could be improved by more suitable housing conditions. A mental or developmental disability was not included in the definition. The Housing Act of 1964 also changed the name of the Section 202 program to "Housing for the Elderly or Handicapped." However, the law did not require that a certain number of units be set aside for tenants with disabilities or direct that units be made accessible. Very few tenants who were considered non-elderly handicapped participated in the Section 202 program between 1964 and 1974. Although data were not collected, HUD estimated that through 1977, less than 1% of Section 202 tenants were non-elderly handicapped,[25] and that "the vast majority of Section 202 projects [were] not designed to serve the handicapped..."[26]

The Housing and Community Development Act of 1974 (P.L. 93-383) removed the word "physical" from the term "physical impairment" in the definition of handicap and also expanded the definition of handicap to include developmental disabilities.[27] The removal of the word “physical” was meant to make persons with mental illnesses eligible for Section 202 housing.[28] However, the development of housing for this population did not occur immediately. In 1978, in the Conference Report accompanying the Housing and Community Development Amendments (P.L. 95-557), Congress acknowledged that “there has been some confusion over whether chronically mentally ill persons are eligible for section 202 housing,” and that it was “never the intent of Congress to exclude chronically mentally ill persons from participating in the section 202 program.”[29] The report went on to direct HUD to develop criteria and standards for providing housing for this population. In 1978, HUD undertook a demonstration program together with the Department of Health and Human Services (then the Department of Health, Education, and Welfare), “to better understand the housing needs of the mentally ill.”[30] In FY1 982, the Section 202 program funded housing for chronically mentally ill individuals for the first time, making funds available for group homes and independent living facilities.[31]

Section 202 Set aside for Non-elderly Handicapped Households

In 1978, the Housing and Community Development Amendments (P.L. 95-557) required that, beginning in FY1 979, at least $50 million of the amounts available for loans under the Section 202 program be devoted to housing for non-elderly “handicapped” individuals.[32] The new requirement was meant to “meet special needs [of the handicapped] which have not been adequately addressed in Section 202 projects.”[33] Until enactment of the Housing and Community Development Amendments of 1978, a small number of accessible units in larger Section 202 developments designed primarily for elderly residents had been dedicated to persons with disabilities (about 1% of units). These Section 202 developments tended to be large multifamily rental buildings — the average number of units in Section 202 developments built prior to enactment of the Housing and Community Development Act of 1974 was 135.[34] HUD suggested that one of the reasons for the low number of units designed for persons with disabilities through the Section 202 program was the additional cost of making units accessible, putting project sponsors at a disadvantage in applying for funds.[35] The set-aside was meant to address this issue.

In addition, P.L. 95-5 57 specified that non-profit sponsors of Section 202 housing were expected to develop innovative ways of providing housing for persons with disabilities, including group homes and independent living complexes integrated into the surrounding community, together with supportive services tailored to resident needs.[36] After enactment of the Housing and Community Development Amendments of 1978 with its set-aside for housing for persons with disabilities, the number of developments built specifically for these households (versus elderly households) increased.[37] HUD estimates that by the end of the 1 980s, approximately 10% of units funded through the Section 202 program were in facilities designed for persons with disabilities.[38]

Nearly ten years after enactment of the Housing and Community Development Amendments, another law made changes to the way in which persons with disabilities were served under the Section 202 program. The Housing and Community Development Act of 1987 (P.L. 100-242) amended the law to require that 15% of the total amount available for Section 202 loans be set aside for persons with disabilities rather than the $50 million established in the 1978 Act (P.L. 95- 557). In appropriations acts from FY1988 through FY1991, Congress went beyond the statutory set aside, however, and required that 25% of Section 202 loan authority be used for housing for persons with disabilities.[39]

Another change made by P.L. 100-242 involved rental subsidies for those Section 202 units for persons with disabilities. Since the enactment of the Housing and Community Development Act of 1974, Section 202 units for both elderly and disabled residents had been subsidized through the project-based Section 8 rental assistance program. However, there was a growing acknowledgment that Section 8 rental assistance was not sufficient to support units for persons with disabilities because it did not take account of the higher cost of providing housing in smaller developments such as group homes.[40] P.L. 100-242 specified that rental assistance in projects for persons with disabilities should be provided through a separate subsidy program based on the "total actual and necessary reasonable costs of developing and operating the project," not including, however, the costs of supportive services.[41] The FY1989 HUD Appropriations Act (P.L. 100-404) provided rental assistance funds for housing for persons with disabilities separately from those for elderly residents. This separate rental assistance was the means of subsidizing Section 202 units for persons with disabilities until the creation of the Section 811 program.[42]

Creation of the Section 811 Program

The incremental separation of housing for persons with disabilities from housing for elderly residents that began in 1978 with a set aside in the Section 202 program and continued with separate rental assistance in 1987 was made permanent in the Cranston-Gonzalez National Affordable Housing Act of 1990 (P.L. 101-625). Congress completely separated housing for persons with disabilities from the Section 202 program by creating the Section 811 Supportive Housing for Persons with Disabilities program.

Not only did P.L. 101-625 separate the housing for persons with disabilities program from the housing for the elderly program, it also changed the way in which units would be financed under both the Section 202 and Section 811 programs. Until the enactment of P.L. 101-625, units created through the Section 202 program had been financed with a combination of loans and project-based Section 8 rental assistance contracts. P.L. 101-625 instituted a method of financing in which Section 202 and Section 811 developments would be financed through capital grants rather than loans. As long as units remain affordable to very low-income residents for at least 40 years, project owners need not repay the capital grants. The law also created a new form of rental assistance similar to Section 8, called PRAC, or project rental assistance contracts. In addition, the law instituted a new way of determining development cost limitations for both Section 202 and Section 811 facilities. The new method was to take account of special design features for persons with disabilities and congregate space for supportive services, among other factors.

The provisions creating the Section 811 program originated in the Senate version of the bill (S. 566) that would become the Cranston-Gonzalez National Affordable Housing Act. The Senate Banking Committee, in its report regarding the bill, described the reasons behind creating a program separate from Section 202:

> The Committee believes that separation of the programs for elderly and persons with disabilities would further the goal of developing a program that meets the housing and related needs of nonelderly persons with disabilities. A separate program would spur the development of a bureaucracy knowledgeable about and sensitive to the special needs of tenants with disabilities, needs which can differ from those of many elderly residents. ... A separate program would also create an institutional voice for housing concerns that are particular to this constituency.[43]

The report also stressed the importance of changing the terminology used to refer to persons served through the Section 811 program, replacing "handicapped persons" with "persons with disabilities."[44] Community integration was another important goal of the new Section 811 program. In the years leading up to the enactment of P.L. 101-625, group homes and other facilities dedicated only to those persons with disabilities had been the focus of housing funded through the Section 202 set aside. Under the Section 811 program, however, the HUD Secretary was to look to a variety of housing options, including scattered units in multifamily housing developments, condominiums, and cooperative housing.

Cranston-Gonzalez authorized capital grants for the new Section 811 program at $271 million for FY1 992 and project rental assistance at $246 million. In FY1 992, Congress funded the new Section 811 program by appropriating $103 million for capital grants and $100 million for new project rental assistance contracts (P.L. 102- 139). The Section 811 program was last authorized from FY2001 through FY2003 at "such sums as necessary" as part of the American Homeownership and Economic Opportunity Act of 2000 (P.L. 106-569). (For recent Section 811 funding levels, see Table 1 at the end of this section.)

Definition of Person with Disabilities in HUD Housing Programs

Resident eligibility for Section 811 housing is based on both income and disability status. The population served by the program, according to the statute, are very low-income persons with disabilities (those with incomes at or below 50% of area median income). Families of persons with disabilities are included in the definition, so that households composed of one or more persons, at least one of whom is an adult with a disability, may be served by the program.[45] The way in which the Section 811 program defines "person with disabilities" differs in some ways from the way HUD defines "person with disabilities" in other programs. This section describes the definition in the Section 811 program, the Section 8 and Public Housing programs, and the Section 202 program. For a table comparing the definitions, see Appendix A.

The Section 811 Program Definition

Under the Section 811 statute, a person with disabilities is defined as an individual having a physical, mental, or emotional impairment: (1) that is expected to be of long-continued and indefinite duration, (2) that substantially impedes his or her ability to live independently, and (3) is of such a nature that the ability to live independently could be improved by more suitable housing conditions.[46] In addition, under the Section 811 statute, persons with developmental disabilities as defined under the Developmental Disabilities and Bill of Rights Act (P.L. 106-402) qualify for Section 811 housing.[47]

The regulations governing Section 811 elaborate further on the definition of "person with disabilities."[48] First, the regulation details what it means to be "developmentally disabled" (described in the section below) and specifies that a person with a "chronic mental illness" that seriously limits his or her ability to live independently and whose impairment could be improved by suitable housing meets the Section 811 definition of person with disabilities. The regulation goes on to state that persons with acquired immunodeficiency virus (HIV), alcoholism, or drug addiction *may* be considered disabled *if* they also have a disability as defined by the Section 811 statute. According to the regulation, "a person whose sole impairment is a diagnosis of HIV positive or alcoholism or drug addiction (i.e., does not meet the qualifying criteria in [the statute]) will not be eligible for occupancy in a section 811 project."[49]

Developmental Disability

According to Section 811 regulations — which mirror the Developmental Disabilities and Bill of Rights Act — a person has a developmental disability if he or she has a severe, chronic disability that (1) is attributable to a physical or mental impairment (or combination of physical and mental impairments); (2) manifests before age 22; (3) is likely to continue indefinitely, and (4) results in substantial functional limitations in at least three major life activities. Life activities are defined as

- self care;
- receptive and expressive language;
- learning;
- mobility;
- self direction;
- capacity for independent living; and

- economic self-sufficiency.

A fifth component of the definition is that the developmental disability reflects the need for individually planned and coordinated care, treatment, or other services for a lifetime or an extended duration.

The Definition in Other HUD Programs

The definition of the term "person with disabilities" in the Section 811 program differs somewhat from the definition for both the Section 8 and Public Housing programs, which are defined together in the same statute and regulation,[50] and properties developed under the Section 202 loan program, which is found in regulation.[51]

While the Section 8/Public Housing definition of person with disabilities includes the Section 811 statutory definition — a physical, mental, or emotional impairment and developmental disabilities — it also adds to the definition persons who are considered disabled under Title II of the Social Security Act.[52] Neither the Section 811 statute nor the regulations governing the program include the Social Security definition of disability. Under the Social Security definition, a person is considered disabled if he or she is unable to work ("engage in any substantial gainful activity") due to a medically determinable physical or mental impairment that is expected to last at least 12 months or to result in death. A person may also be considered disabled under the Social Security Act definition if he or she is age 55 or older, is blind, and is unable to engage in substantial gainful activity.[53]

The statute governing disability under Section 8 and Public Housing further specifies that the term person with disabilities "shall not exclude" those living with acquired immunodeficiency syndrome (AIDS) or conditions arising from its etiologic agent. Unlike the Section 811 regulation, the Section 8/Public Housing definition does not exclude persons whose only diagnosis is that of HIV positive. However, the Section 8/Public Housing regulation is similar to the Section 811 regulation in stating that an individual shall not be considered a person with disabilities based *solely* on drug or alcohol dependence.

The term "handicapped person or individual" for purposes of facilities developed with Section 202 loans[54] — which contain units for persons with disabilities — is defined in regulation. The Section 202 program definition is very similar to the Section 811 definition, and differs only in the way in which it describes a person who is infected with HIV/AIDS. According to the regulation, those who are infected with HIV, and who are disabled as a result of the infection, are eligible for housing built through the Section 202 loan program. The type of housing for which those individuals would be eligible, according to the regulation, depends upon the nature of the person's disability — i.e. housing that is designed for persons with physical disabilities, developmental disabilities, or chronic mental illnesses. Finally, like the law and regulations governing Section 811, Section 8, and Public Housing, Section 202 regulations make ineligible any person whose "sole impairment" is alcoholism or drug addiction.

Capital Grants and Project Rental Assistance

Most Section 811 funding is distributed as capital grants and project rental assistance to nonprofit housing sponsors (the program also funds tenant-based vouchers, described in the next section). With the capital grants, nonprofit grantees build or rehabilitate housing to be used for persons with disabilities and their families. HUD distributes the Section 811 capital grants through a two-step process. First, a formula is used to allocate available funds to the 51 local HUD offices based on the number of non-institutionalized persons within the jurisdiction of the local office who are between 16 and 64 years of age and have a disability.[55] Each of the 51 jurisdictions is ensured funding sufficient to support a minimum of ten Section 811 units. HUD then awards Section 811 grants through a competitive process in which nonprofit organizations submit applications, and awards are limited by the amount allocated to the local office.

Grantees need not pay back the capital grants as long as the property remains affordable to very low-income tenants with disabilities (those with incomes at or below 50% of area median income) for at least 40 years.[56] The project sponsors also receive rental assistance from HUD to make up the difference between the rent paid by residents and the costs of operating the housing development. In addition, project sponsors must ensure that residents in Section 811 housing receive appropriate supportive services. As of 2007, HUD reported that a total of 26,656 units had been built with Section 811 capital grants and were receiving rental assistance.[57] This section of the report describes these components of the Section 811 program.

Eligible Facilities

The Section 811 statute governs the type of housing that may be provided through the program, but in some cases, the statutory definitions have been further refined through HUD regulation and policy. The physical design of Section 811 housing may take on several forms:[58]

- *Group Home:* The Section 811 statute defines a group home as a single-family residence designed for occupancy by not more than eight individuals with disabilities. However, HUD's annual Notice of Funding Availability (NOFA) that guides applicants for Section 811 funds specifies that no more than six individuals with disabilities may live in a group home.[59] Bedrooms may be single or double occupancy, but in the latter case, only when requested by the residents.[60] There must be at least one bathroom for every four residents,[61] and an additional bedroom may be provided for a staff person.[62] Project sponsors may not place more than one group home on a single site or on a site adjacent to another group home.[63]
- *Independent Living Facility:* According to the Section 811 statute, an independent living facility has individual dwelling units with separate bedrooms, kitchens, and baths for each resident, with a maximum occupancy of 24 persons with disabilities per development (higher numbers may be allowed with approval from HUD).[64] However, the Section 811 NOFA further restricts the maximum number of persons in an independent living facility to 14 with some exceptions allowed.[65] The independent living units may be located on scattered sites, and a unit may be provided for a staff person.[66]
- *Condominium Projects:* Condominium units are similar to independent living facilities, with separate bedrooms, baths and kitchens for each resident. Standards for condominium units under the Section 811 program are not provided in statute or regulation, but are outlined in the annual HUD NOFA. The maximum number of units allowed on a site or scattered sites is the greater of 14 units or 10% of units in a development, not to exceed 24 units.[67] Unlike independent living facilities, a unit may not be used by a staff person.

Project sponsors may choose to serve residents that fall within one of three major disability categories — physical disability, developmental disability, and chronic mental illness — or any combination of the three.[68] In addition, with HUD approval, project sponsors may further restrict residency to a subcategory of disability that falls within one of these three categories. For example, a group house dedicated to individuals with developmental disabilities could choose specifically to serve those persons with autism (with HUD's consent). However, if HUD approves the restriction, a project sponsor cannot deny occupancy to an otherwise qualified applicant who meets the definition of the broader disability category.[69] For example, in the case of a group home for persons with autism, the owners could not deny a qualified application from a person with another developmental disability, but could deny a qualified application from a person with a physical disability. In order to qualify to restrict residency by categories of disability, applicants for Section 811 funds must explain why it is necessary to restrict residency, and why it is not possible to serve residents in a more integrated setting.[70]

Rental Assistance

Nonprofit organizations that are awarded capital grants to build or rehabilitate Section 811 housing facilities also enter into contracts with HUD to receive project rental assistance (referred to as PRAC). The rental assistance is paid to project sponsors by HUD in order to make up the difference between the rent paid by tenants and the cost of operating the Section 811 housing facility.[71] Residents in Section 811 housing must be "very low income" (with income at or below 50% of area median income),[72] and they pay the higher of 30% of their adjusted income or 10% of their gross income toward rent.[73] The initial term of PRAC contracts is three years, and they are renewable on an annual basis subject to appropriations.

Supportive Services

Housing developed through Section 811 capital grants must be supportive housing, that is, owners must make supportive services available to residents to help them live independently. Supportive housing is a model used to assist a variety of populations for whom it might be difficult to maintain housing, not just persons with disabilities. These groups include elderly residents, families with young children whose parents are making the transition to work, formerly homeless individuals, and those living with HIV/AIDS. Services are to be tailored to the individual needs of residents and so depend upon the population being served. Specifically, the Section 811 statute requires property owners to ensure the availability of supportive services to address the health (including mental health), and other individual needs of residents.[74] However, Section 811 funds cannot themselves be used to fund supportive services for residents.[75] Owners may provide supportive services directly to residents, or may coordinate the availability of services through outside agencies or service providers. Services may include assistance with activities of daily living; counseling for mental health issues, drug, or alcohol addictions; case management; and employment assistance.

When organizations apply to HUD for Section 811 capital grants, they must submit a supportive services plan that has been certified by the appropriate state or local agency responsible for overseeing services to persons with disabilities as being well-designed to serve the needs of the prospective residents.[76] The supportive services plans must include the following information (among other requirements): (1) a detailed description of the service needs of the population that will be served; (2) a list of community service providers that will provide services, and letters of intent from those providers; (3) the experience of the proposed service providers; (4) a description of how state and local agencies will be involved in the project; and (5) the applicant's commitment to provide services for residents.[77] While project sponsors are required to ensure that supportive services are available, they cannot require residents to accept them.

Tenant-Based Vouchers

Tenant-based rental assistance allows individuals and families to find rental housing on the private market rather than in specific housing developments. The rental assistance goes with the tenant rather than being tied to a specific housing unit. Rental assistance is provided in the form of a voucher, through which HUD pays a portion of a tenant's rent to landlords who are willing to accept the voucher (federal law does not require landlords to accept vouchers). The Section 8 voucher program is the primary way in which HUD provides tenant-based rental assistance, although tenant-based assistance is available through other programs, including Section 811.[78] In both programs, tenants with vouchers pay between 30% and 40% of their income toward rent and HUD pays the difference between the family's contribution and the rent for the unit, subject to certain limits.

This section of the report describes Section 811 vouchers for persons with disabilities; Section 8 vouchers for persons with disabilities are described later in the report. (For more information about the Section 8 program, see CRS Report RL32284, *An Overview of the Section 8 Housing Programs*, by Maggie McCarty.)

Section 811 Mainstream Vouchers

The Housing and Community Development Act of 1992 (P.L. 102-550) made tenant-based rental assistance part of the Section 811 program by authorizing the use of vouchers for eligible households.[79] The vouchers, sometimes referred to as "mainstream vouchers," are administered using the same rules that govern the Section 8 voucher program. Unlike Section 8 vouchers, however, these vouchers are funded through the Section 811 account for initial five-year terms (Section 8 vouchers are funded on an annual basis). The first year in which Congress set aside funding for mainstream vouchers was FY1997. The HUD Appropriations Act for that year (P.L. 104-204) specified that HUD could use up to 25% of the amount appropriated for the Section 811 program for five-year vouchers.

In the first two years that the Section 811 vouchers were distributed, only public housing authorities (PHAs) could administer the vouchers, but beginning in FY1 999, private nonprofit organizations were eligible to apply to administer them.[80] HUD makes vouchers available through an annual Notice of Funding Availability (NOFA) process through which PHAs and private nonprofit organizations interested in administering the vouchers apply to HUD. Applicants are scored based on a number of factors, which include the number of persons with disabilities at or below poverty in the area to be served by the applicant as well as the existence of agreements with organizations that will provide supportive services to voucher holders.[81] Since 2005, HUD has required voucher administrators (PHAs and private nonprofit organizations) to help persons with disabilities who have Section 811 vouchers to obtain supportive services if they request them, as well as to provide technical assistance to landlords in making reasonable accommodations or reasonable modifications.[82]

The NOFAs issued by HUD in FY1 997-FY1 999 specified that the Section 811 vouchers should remain available to disabled families during the initial funding term of the voucher (five years), but were silent on who could use the voucher if the original family left the program (either voluntarily or due to eviction or other non- voluntary reason) after the initial funding period was over. Advocates for persons with disabilities have pointed out that these vouchers may have been provided to non-disabled households after the original tenant left the program.[83] However, in annual appropriations acts since FY2005, Congress has required that Section 811 vouchers be made available to disabled families upon turnover.[84] Further, in 2004, HUD began to require that PHAs track the disability status of families using Section 811 vouchers and provide the records to HUD.[85] Prior to 2004, HUD did not collect this information. As of 2007, HUD reported that a total of 14,836 Section 811 vouchers were funded through the Section 811 account.[86]

Table 1. Section 811 Funding Levels, FY2003 to FY2008 (dollars in thousands)

Fiscal Year	Section 811 Capital Grants and PRAC[a]	Section 811 Vouchers[b]	Total for Section 811[c]
2003	166,787	81,851	248,886
2004	173,721	74,904	249,092
2005	149,455	88,179	238,080
2006	152,603	78,269	231,268
2007	158,697	77,517	236,610
2008	161,655	74,745	237,000

Source: Department of Housing and Urban Development Budget Justifications FY2005 through FY2009.

[a] PRAC refers to "project-based rental assistance contracts." Amounts for PRAC include renewals of existing contracts as well as rental assistance for new units.

[s] Amounts for Section 811 vouchers include funds to renew existing vouchers.

[c] The total may be slightly greater than the sum of funds allocated for capital grants, PRAC, and vouchers due to funds appropriated for the working capital fund that are included in the total.

OTHER HUD HOUSING DESIGNATED FOR PERSONS WITH DISABILITIES

While the Section 811 program is dedicated solely to persons with disabilities, HUD also funds housing for persons with disabilities through programs that serve all tenant populations, but that also give project owners the ability to designate buildings to special populations, including elderly persons and persons with disabilities.[87] In addition to housing historically provided through the Section 202 program (described in the "Evolution of Section 811" section of this report), property owners that participate in the project-based Section 8 rental assistance program and Public Housing Authorities (PHAs) that administer the Public Housing program may choose to designate buildings specifically for elderly residents and residents with disabilities together (sometimes referred to as "mixed population" developments) or for residents with disabilities alone. In addition, the Section 8 voucher program sets aside housing vouchers specifically for persons with disabilities.

Public Housing

Public housing is the original federally assisted housing program for low-income families, created as part of the Housing Act of 1937 (P.L. 75-412). The program provides housing for very low-income households (those with incomes at or below 50% of area median income) and requires tenants to pay 30% of their income toward rent. The Housing Act of 1956 (P.L. 84-1020) authorized the Public Housing Administration (a predecessor to HUD) to provide units specifically for low- income elderly individuals.[88] The first elderly-only public housing development was built by 1960.[89] Beginning in 1961, the HUD definition of "elderly family" was amended to include individuals with disabilities of any age.[90] Since then, persons with disabilities have lived in public housing facilities designated for elderly residents (defined as households where one or more person is age 62 or older).

Public housing developments designated for elderly residents, and where a mixed population of elderly residents and residents with disabilities live together, have been controversial. During the early years of public housing for elderly persons, disabled residents made up only a small proportion of residents. The number of residents with disabilities living in public housing for the elderly began to increase in the 1 980s and early 1 990s for at least two reasons. First, individuals with mental illnesses were less likely to be institutionalized as a result of the availability of outpatient mental health care, and were therefore in need of affordable housing.[91] A second factor was passage of the 1988 Fair Housing Act Amendments (P.L. 100- 430). The amendments added persons with a "handicap" to the class of individuals protected from discrimination in the provision of housing. The definition of "handicap" included individuals with alcohol and drug addictions.[92] Following these changes, Public Housing experienced an increase in the number of younger residents with disabilities, often with mental illnesses and addictions. Along with the increase, Public Housing Authorities reported a greater number of incidents of disruptive behavior, and some elderly residents reported feeling unsafe.[93]

Due to tension between elderly residents and residents with disabilities, in the Housing and Community Development Act of 1992 (P.L. 102-550) Congress allowed PHAs to designate buildings as elderly only, disabled only, or as mixed population facilities.[94] In 1996, The Public Housing Opportunity Extension Act of 1996 (P.L. 104-120) streamlined the process for designating public housing projects. If a PHA wants to change the composition of a building to elderly residents only or to residents with disabilities, it must submit a plan to HUD to ask for approval. If the plan is approved, PHAs cannot evict non-eligible residents. For example, if a PHA designates a building with a mix of elderly residents and residents with disabilities as elderly only, tenants with disabilities may not be evicted. If tenants want to move, however, PHAs may help them relocate. According to HUD data, of the 180 Public Housing projects that are designated for elderly tenants, tenants with disabilities, or both populations together, 25 projects set aside units for tenants with disabilities.[95]

Project-Based Section 8 Rental Assistance

Between 1974 and 1983, the Section 8 new construction and substantial rehabilitation program made rental assistance available to developers that were creating new and rehabilitated rental housing for low-income families.[96] From the inception of the program, owners were able to develop properties designated for use by elderly residents together with tenants with disabilities. The Housing and Community Development Act of 1992 (P.L. 102-550) gave owners of properties designed primarily for occupancy by mixed populations — elderly families together with tenants with disabilities — the ability to establish a preference for elderly families when selecting tenants.[97] However, unlike Public Housing, most Section 8 properties may not completely exclude residents with disabilities. The statute requires owners that choose to create a preference for elderly residents to continue to reserve some units for households where an adult member has a disability and where the household is not considered elderly or near elderly (defined as at least 50 years old but below the age of 62[98]). Specifically, owners are required to set aside the lower of the number of units occupied by disabled families in 1 992[99] or 10% of units. If owners are unable to rent the units reserved for elderly residents to eligible families, they may give a preference to near elderly families with an adult member who has a disability.[100] If owners are unable to rent units designated for non-elderly and non-near elderly persons with disabilities, they may rent them to near elderly persons with disabilities.

Section 8 Vouchers for Persons with Disabilities

In addition to housing vouchers made available through the Section 811 program (described earlier in this report), HUD has set aside Section 8 vouchers for families with an adult member who has a disability. The voucher portion of the Section 8 program was created in 1983 as part of the Supplemental Appropriations Act of 1984 (P.L. 98-181). Unlike project-based Section 8 rental assistance, which is tied to specific rental units, tenants may use Section 8 vouchers to rent any eligible housing unit. To be eligible, a unit must meet minimum housing quality standards and a family's portion of the rent cannot exceed 40% of their income.[101] In addition, a landlord must agree to accept the voucher.[102]

Congress appropriated funds for Section 8 vouchers for persons with disabilities, sometimes referred to as "designated housing vouchers," in response to enactment of the Housing and Community Development Act of 1992 (P.L. 102-550). As discussed earlier, provisions in P.L. 102-550 permitted owners of Public Housing and project-based Section 8 developments where elderly residents and residents with disabilities lived together to either designate buildings as elderly only or to prioritize elderly tenants.[103] Section 8 owners were given the authority to create a preference for elderly families in these designated buildings, though they could not exclude disabled families altogether. PHAs were given the authority to designate entire buildings as elderly only. Although PHAs cannot evict tenants with disabilities if a building is designated as elderly only, with attrition, eventually a building may have only elderly residents. These policy changes affected the ability of tenants with disabilities to live in these facilities.

From FY1997 through FY2002, Congress appropriated funds for Section 8 vouchers in order to assist tenants with disabilities who would have been eligible to reside in those Section 8 and Public Housing developments prior to their designation as elderly only or elderly preference. PHAs applied for these designated housing vouchers, which they then provided to eligible tenants. In FY2008, for the first time since FY2002, Congress appropriated additional funds for designated housing vouchers.[104] The FY2008 Consolidated Appropriations Act (P.L. 110-161) provided $30 million for Section 8 vouchers for tenants with disabilities affected by the designation or restriction of tenant populations to elderly only.

Unlike Section 811 mainstream vouchers, Section 8 designated housing vouchers for persons with disabilities shall remain available to other disabled households upon turnover "*to the extent practicable* [emphasis added]."[105] (Section 811 vouchers must be made available *only* to families where an adult member has a disability.) HUD defines the term "to the extent practicable" to mean that before a voucher can be provided to a non-disabled household, every eligible non-elderly disabled family on a PHA's waiting list must have received a voucher, and that outreach must not have resulted in finding an eligible family.[106] As with Section 811 vouchers, PHAs must assist tenants who request help in finding supportive services, and provide technical assistance to landlords in providing reasonable accommodations and modifications.

Housing Financed by Low-Income Housing Tax Credits and HUD Block Grants

Beginning in the 1980s, the federal government took a less direct role in the development of affordable housing. At the same time, the production and rehabilitation of housing at the state and local level began to increase.[107] This occurred, in part, due to the enactment of the Low-Income Housing Tax Credit (LIHTC) and the HOME Investment Partnerships program. These programs distribute funds to states and localities for the production of affordable housing. States and localities may, in turn, decide to target a portion of the funds from these programs to develop affordable housing for persons with disabilities. This section of the report describes the LIHTC and the HOME program, as well as the Community Development Block Grant (CDBG), a program created in 1974 to assist states and localities with economic development, including housing activities that benefit low- and moderate-income households.

The Low-Income Housing Tax Credit

The Low-Income Housing Tax Credit (LIHTC) was enacted as part of the Tax Reform Act of 1986 (P.L. 99-514). The program provides incentives for the development of affordable rental housing through federal tax credits administered by the Internal Revenue Service (IRS). The IRS allocates tax credits to states based on population, and states award the credits to developers to use as a source of financing for the development of affordable rental housing.[108]

The states, generally through their state housing finance agencies (HFAs), award the tax credits to housing developers through a competitive process that is based on state priorities as set out annually in their Qualified Allocation Plan (QAP). Developers may either retain the credits themselves or sell them in exchange for equity to fund a housing development. Developers of LIHTC - financed housing must ensure that at least 40% of the units are affordable to households with incomes at or below 60% of the area median income, or that at least 20% of units are affordable to households with incomes at or below 50% of the area median income.[109] The projects must remain affordable for at least 15 years, although there are incentives in place to encourage developers to maintain affordability for 30 years. Rent charged for the rent-restricted units in a development may not exceed 30% of an imputed income limitation — calculated based on area median incomes.

In their Qualified Allocation Plans, states set forth the criteria they will use in selecting projects to receive the tax credits.[110] By statute, states must prioritize LIHTC projects that serve the lowest income tenants for the longest period of time in their QAPs. In addition, the LIHTC statute requires states to consider certain criteria in determining how they will set housing priorities in the QAP. One of the ten criteria that states must consider is tenant populations with special needs.[111] Tenant populations with special needs may include persons with disabilities (others with special needs include individuals and families who are homeless, elderly individuals, or other populations in need of housing with supportive services).[112]

States may choose to make housing units for populations with special needs one of the priorities in the competition for tax credits in a number of ways.[113] These methods include:

- requiring developers to set aside a portion of units for special needs populations — for example, North Carolina requires that the greater of five units or 10% of units in each tax credit development be devoted to persons with disabilities or those who are homeless;[114]
- setting aside a certain dollar value or percentage of available tax credits for a specified population — for example, Illinois sets aside $2 million of the total available tax credits for developments where at least 50% of units serve persons with special needs;[115]
- developing a scoring system in the competition for tax credits that awards additional points for proposals that take account of certain special needs populations — for example, New Mexico awards 15 points in the tax credit competition to developers that propose to build housing in which at least 25% of units are dedicated to persons with special needs.[116]

The HOME Investment Partnerships Program

The HOME Investment Partnerships program (referred to as the HOME program) is a block grant to states and local jurisdictions — referred to as "participating jurisdictions" — distributed via a formula for the purpose of developing both affordable rental housing and affordable housing for homeowners.[117] The factors used to distribute HOME funds to eligible states and jurisdictions include population, the number of rental units occupied by households in poverty, housing overcrowding, the number of units with incomplete kitchens or plumbing, and the age of housing.[118] HOME funds can be used to build or rehabilitate housing, to provide tenant-based rental assistance, and to provide assistance to homeowners and homebuyers. Assistance must go to low-income households (at least 90% of funds must assist those with incomes at or below 60% of area median income), and any housing provided must be affordable.

Like funds provided to states through the LIHTC, states and localities that receive HOME funds have discretion in choosing the populations they wish to serve. Also like the LIHTC, jurisdictions that receive HOME funds develop a plan regarding how they will distribute funds. This is done through HUD's Consolidated Plan process. Jurisdictions applying for funds from four HUD formula grant programs, including HOME,[119] submit a single Consolidated Plan to HUD. The plan includes an assessment of community needs and a proposal to address those needs, using both federal funds and community resources. State and local plans must also contain a housing needs assessment, including the need for housing for persons with disabilities.[120] In developing the plan, states and communities must adopt a citizen participation plan, through which they are encouraged to consult with citizens with disabilities.[121] States are further required to consult with organizations that provide services (including fair housing services) to persons with disabilities when preparing their consolidated plan.[122]

After taking into consideration the needs of persons with disabilities, HOME recipient jurisdictions may choose to prioritize housing for persons with disabilities as part of their Consolidated Plans.[123] In the tenant-based rental assistance portion of the program, the HOME regulations specify that recipient jurisdictions may choose to establish a preference for tenants with special needs, including persons with disabilities.[124] Further, recipients of HOME funds may choose to target tenant-based rental assistance to individuals with a specific disability. In terms of new or rehabilitated rental housing that may be developed with HOME funds, communities can choose to develop not only multifamily rental housing and single family homes, but also transitional housing, single room occupancy projects, and group homes.[125] Some jurisdictions may find that these types of housing developments are well suited for tenants with disabilities.

The Community Development Block Grant Program

The Community Development Block Grant (CDBG) program was enacted as part of the Housing Act of 1974 (P.L. 93-383) with the purpose of developing viable urban communities by funding housing, community, and economic development activities that principally benefit low- and moderate-income households.[126] The CDBG program distributes 70% of total funds through formula grants to entitlement communities — central cities of metropolitan areas, cities with populations of 50,000 or more, and urban counties — and the remaining 30% goes to states for use in small, non-entitlement communities.[127] The allocation of CDBG funds is determined through a formula that targets an area's need for community development using a variety of factors including population, poverty, overcrowded housing, age of housing, and the lag in community growth.[128] The CDBG program is subject to the same Consolidated Plan requirements as the HOME program (described previously) in which the needs of persons with disabilities must be taken into consideration. In addition, in response to the Bush Administration's New Freedom Initiative, HUD issued guidance to assist CDBG recipients with "identifying the needs of persons with disabilities and targeting CDBG resources to meet those needs during the development of the jurisdictions' consolidated plans."[129]

While many of the purposes of CDBG funds involve the improvement of neighborhoods, the creation of public facilities, or the promotion of economic opportunity, funds may also be used to rehabilitate housing, including making housing accessible for persons with disabilities. CDBG funds may also be used to make public facilities accessible to persons with disabilities.[130] In addition, communities may use CDBG funds for "public services," which include such services as employment counseling. According to HUD, promoting economic opportunities for persons with disabilities through job training and employment counseling are valid uses of CDBG funds.[131]

Issues and Trends

Using Section 811 Funds with Low-Income Housing Tax Credits

Financing affordable housing, including housing for persons with disabilities, may require multiple streams of funding in order to support the design, construction, and ongoing operating costs of a project. In addition to federal funds provided through HUD programs, affordable housing developers may use mortgage revenue bonds, tax credits, and local housing trust fund resources, among other sources, to develop housing for low-income and special needs populations. While HUD funds once might have been sufficient on their own to develop an affordable housing project, that is rarely the case today. This is true for Section 811 developers, who often must bring together multiple sources of funding to develop a project. In 2000, in order to help Section 811 (and Section 202) developers bring together multiple financing sources, Congress enacted a law that makes the interaction of Section 811 funds and the Low-Income Housing Tax Credits (LIHTCs) more feasible by changing the definition of "private nonprofit organization" in the Section 811 statute. This change, and its implication for Section 811 developers, is described below.

The value of LIHTCs are determined, in part, based on the cost of developing a property — referred to as the qualified basis.[132] The costs of constructing, acquiring, and rehabilitating a property (among other costs[133]) are included in calculating the qualified basis, but the amount must then be reduced by any federal grants received by the developer, which in turn reduces the value of the tax credits. Therefore, if a nonprofit developer were to receive a Section 811 capital grant, its value would be subtracted in calculating the qualified basis which could result in minimal LIHTCs. The Homeownership and Economic Opportunity Act (P.L. 106-569), enacted in 2000, allowed for-profit limited partnerships, where a nonprofit organization is the sole general partner, to be eligible Section 811 owners. The changed law allows a nonprofit Section 811 grantee to loan the Section 811 capital grant to the limited partnership. Under this arrangement, the Section 811 funds are no longer a "federal grant" to be subtracted in calculating the qualified basis, potentially increasing the value of LIHTCs.

The change in the law to allow for-profit limited partnerships to own Section 811 housing developments has not immediately made mixed financing arrangements common, however. The transactions are complicated and may require extensive expertise in housing finance to make them work. HUD acknowledges that "most developers seek to avoid the use of federal grant financing in most LIHTC projects."[134] In addition, the treatment of Section 811 PRAC in tax credit transactions has been unclear. Although the IRS has created exceptions to the rule that federal grants do not count toward the qualified basis of a property for certain categories of rental assistance, Section 811 PRAC has not been among the exceptions. The programs that have been exempted from the requirement include Section 8 project-based rental assistance payments and public housing capital and operating funds,[135] the Native American Housing Block Grant Program,[136] Rent Supplement and Rental Assistance Payments programs,[137] and the Shelter Plus Care and Single

Room Occupancy programs.[138] Despite language in the Homeownership and Economic Opportunity Act of 2000 indicating that Congress intended Section 811 (and Section 202) assistance to be included in calculating qualified basis (rather than subtracted from it), the IRS has not issued a ruling that would be necessary to make this possible.[139]

Another possible limitation in developing mixed finance projects using federal grants such as Section 811 together with the LIHTC was removed with passage of the Housing and Economic Recovery Act of 2008 (P.L. 110-289). Under LIHTC law, developers may qualify for tax credits worth roughly 9% or 4%.[140] Under previous LIHTC law, the higher 9% credit was available for new construction that was *not* federally subsidized, while the 4% credit was available for either federally subsidized new construction or existing buildings. The statutory definition of "federally subsidized" included below market federal loans (the structure used by limited partnerships to loan Section 811 capital grants).[141] The fact that developers of federally subsidized buildings did not qualify for the higher tax credit made financing projects with the LIHTC less lucrative. Developers either had to accept the lower, 4% credit, or to set up a system through which federal grants were loaned to the project at a market rate of interest.[142]

However, P.L. 110-289 removed the phrase "below market federal loans" from the definition of federal subsidy in the LIHTC statute. This makes all federally subsidized new construction placed in service after the effective date of P.L. 110-289 eligible for 9% tax credits. The 9% credits are very competitive,[143] however, and it may still be difficult for Section 811 developers to obtain them.

Housing Need for Persons with Disabilities

According to both advocates for persons with disabilities and HUD, persons with disabilities have a need for affordable housing. Since 1991, HUD has regularly released reports (ten to date) on the worst case needs for affordable housing in the United States.[144] HUD defines households with worst case housing needs as very low-income renter households (those households with incomes at or below 50% of area median income) that do not receive rental assistance and either (1) pay more than half their income toward rent, or (2) live in severely substandard housing.[145] Substandard housing is measured using the American Housing Survey definition of housing with severe physical problems. These are varying degrees of problems with plumbing, heating, electrical wiring, and upkeep of the physical unit or public areas.[146] Using data from the 2005 American Housing Survey, in its most recent report — *Affordable Housing Needs 2005* — HUD found that 5.99 million households had worst case housing needs, a statistically significant increase of 16% over the 5.18 million households that had worst case needs in 2003. [147] This represented an increase from 4.89% of all U.S. households to 5.50% of all households.

The *Affordable Housing Needs 2005* report also included an estimate of the number of persons with disabilities who have worst case housing needs. Because disability status is not reported in the American Housing Survey, HUD used three sources of income as proxies to estimate households where a non-elderly adult member has a disability. These three proxies were: (1) Social Security and Railroad Retirement Benefits, (2) Supplemental Security Income (SSI), and (3) public assistance such as welfare. Using these three income sources as proxies, HUD estimated that there were 542,000 households with a non-elderly adult member with a disability that had worst case housing needs.[148] These estimates did not include households with children.

Less than a year after releasing the *Affordable Housing Needs 2005* report, however, HUD released a supplement in which it revised the estimate of households with a non-elderly adult who has a disability and that has worst case housing needs.[149] The supplement used an additional income proxy to arrive at an increased number of persons with disabilities with worst case housing needs over the number that had been estimated in the original report. In addition to Social Security/Railroad Retirement benefits, SSI, and public assistance, the supplemental report included cases where respondents to the American Housing Survey reported that they received Social Security Disability Insurance (SSDI), workers' compensation, veterans' disability payments, or other disability payments.

Using these four income sources as a proxy for disability status, the HUD supplement estimated the number of households having a non-elderly adult member with a disability in two different categories: those households with children, and those without children. (The original *Affordable Housing Needs 2005* report did not report the number of households with children and an adult with a disability.) Of very low-income households without children and an adult with a disability, HUD reported that 694,000 had worst case housing needs, making up 11.6% of all households with worst case housing needs (the original estimate in the *Affordable Housing Needs 2005* report was 542,000). Of those very low-income households with children and an adult with a disability, the supplement estimated that 365,000 had worst case housing needs, making up 6.1% of all households with worst case housing needs. Nonetheless, HUD noted that even its updated estimates are an undercount of persons with disabilities who have worst case housing needs.[150] This is due to the fact that homeowners, homeless persons, and persons living in institutions are not part of the worst case needs calculation.

The HUD supplement to its *Affordable Housing Needs 2005* report was in part in response to an analysis commissioned by the Consortium for Citizens with Disabilities (CCD) Housing Task Force, a coalition of groups that advocates for persons with disabilities.[151] The CCD report, whose author had been an author on previous HUD *Affordable Housing Needs* reports, like the HUD supplement, used the fourth income proxy — SSDI, workers' compensation, veterans' disability or other disability benefits — for estimating disability status. Unlike the HUD methodology, however, the CCD report used as an adjustment factor data on persons with disabilities from two other surveys, the Survey of Income and Program Participation and the National Health Interview Survey. According to the CCD report, these two surveys ask more questions about disability than the American Housing Survey. Using these adjusted data, the CCD report estimated that between 1.3 and 1.4 million childless non-elderly adults with disabilities had worst case housing needs, while between 840,000 and 960,000 households with children and a non-elderly adult with a disability had worst case housing needs.[152]

Homeless Persons with Disabilities

Although homelessness in the United States has always existed, it became a more prevalent phenomenon in the 1 970s and 1 980s, when the homeless population began to grow and become more visible to the general public. Explanations for the growth in homelessness include the demolition of skid rows,[153] the decreased availability of affordable housing generally, the reduced need for seasonal unskilled labor, the reduced likelihood that relatives will accommodate homeless family members, the decreased value of public benefits, and changed admissions standards at mental hospitals.[154]

Early in the current decade, attention was again turned to homeless individuals, this time to those persons who experience so-called “chronic homelessness,” when President Bush announced an initiative to end chronic homelessness within ten years. In the late 1 990s, researchers identified chronically homeless individuals as those who have a disability (including those who suffer from mental illness and/or substance abuse disorders) and who have been homeless for long periods of time.[155] According to HUD, a person is chronically homeless if they have been continuously homeless for one year or have experienced four episodes of homelessness in the past three years.[156] Estimates of the number of chronically homeless individuals as a percentage of the total homeless population range from 18% to 27%.[157] Rates of mental health problems are estimated to exist in more than 60% of chronically homeless individuals, and more than 80% of individuals are estimated to have alcohol or drug problems.[158] Medical problems, including HIV/AIDS, are also prevalent among chronically homeless individuals.[159]

Communities across the country have addressed chronic homelessness through a strategy called “housing first,” in which permanent supportive housing is found for homeless individuals prior to treatment of their illnesses and addictions. HUD makes funds available through its Homeless Assistance Grants for the construction or rehabilitation of new permanent supportive housing for chronically homeless individuals.[160] In the first four years after the announcement of President Bush’s initiative to end chronic homelessness, an estimated 37,500 new permanent supportive housing units were added to the stock of housing available for homeless individuals with disabilities.[161]

Legislation

The Frank Melville Supportive Housing Investment Act (H.R. 5772)

A bill to amend the Section 811 program, the Frank Melville Supportive Housing Investment Act of 2008 (H.R. 5772) was introduced in the House on April 10, 2008. On July 30, 2008, the bill was approved by the House Financial Services Committee, and on September 17, 2008, it passed the full House under suspension of the rules. A similar bill with the same title was introduced in the Senate on September 25, 2008 (S. 3593).

H.R. 5772 would make a number of changes to the Section 811 program. One of these would be to eliminate the funding of tenant-based rental assistance through the Section 811 program account. Advocates for persons with disabilities contend that Section 811 vouchers are poorly targeted and may not always be used to serve households with disabilities.[162] Instead, existing and future vouchers would be funded through the Section 8 account. The bill would authorize sufficient Section 8 funds to support the number of vouchers that were funded in FY2008. H.R. 5772 also would codify the requirement that Congress has inserted in recent appropriations acts requiring Section 811 vouchers to be turned over to households where an adult member has a disability when the current voucher holders give them up.

Another proposed change would reduce the concentration of persons with disabilities in Section 811-funded housing by limiting the number of units in a building developed with Section 811 capital grants to 25% of the total units in the building. Limiting the number of units for persons with disabilities in a building would also encourage developers to use other funding sources, such as the Low Income Housing Tax Credit (LIHTC) to supplement the Section 811 funding. This 25% limitation would not apply to group homes or independent living facilities. In cases where grantees combine Section 811 capital grants with funding from other sources such as LIHTCs for the development of multifamily housing, the bill would delegate the review and processing of the project to state or local housing finance agencies (HFAs). Because HFAs are the agencies that administer tax credits, delegating the processing of the Section 811 capital grant to the HFA, together with the tax credit, is thought to be more efficient.

In addition, H.R. 5772 would create a Project Rental Assistance-Only Competitive Demonstration Program to encourage mixed finance developments where rental units for persons with disabilities would be interspersed with units for non-disabled households. The rental assistance awarded through the demonstration program, instead of subsidizing units developed through Section 811 capital grants, would be used to subsidize units of housing developed through LIHTCs, the HOME program, or projects developed with government funds from other sources. Under the demonstration program, only extremely low-income persons with disabilities would be eligible for the assisted units (those with incomes at or below 30% of area median income) and no more than 25% of units in LIHTC and HOME developments would be allowed to be set-aside for those households. The initial term of the rental assistance would be 15 years, although facilities would be required to operate for at least 30 years as supportive housing for persons with disabilities.

The bill also would amend the definition of "person with disabilities" in the Section 811 program to include a person who meets the Social Security Act definition of disability. As noted earlier in this report, the current Section 811 definition does not reference the Social Security definition. In addition, the bill would expand the Section 811 definition to include those individuals who are living with HIV/AIDS consistent with the Public Housing and Section 8 programs. (See Appendix A.) Current Section 811 regulations state that a "person whose sole impairment is a diagnosis of HIV positive ... (i.e. does not meet the qualifying criteria in [the statute]) will not be eligible for occupancy in a section 811 project." The proposed language would instead state that the term person with disabilities "shall not exclude persons who have the disease of acquired immunodeficiency syndrome or any conditions arising from the etiologic agent for acquired immunodeficiency syndrome." H.R. 5772 also would make clear that persons age 62 and older may not be considered a "person with disabilities" for purposes of the Section 811 program.

APPENDIX A. DEFINITIONS OF DISABILITY APPLICABLE TO HUD HOUSING PROGRAMS

Table A-1. Definitions of Disability Applicable to HUD Housing Programs

Provision	Section 811	Section 8 and Public Housing	Section 202 Loan Program
Mental, Physical, or Emotional Impairment	A physical, mental, or emotional impairment that is (1) expected to be of long-continued and indefinite duration, (2) substantially impedes a person's ability to live independently, and (3) could be improved by more suitable housing conditions.	Same.	Same.
Chronic Mental Illness	*A severe and persistent mental or emotional impairment.*	*No Provision*	*Same as Section 811.*
Developmental Disability	A severe, chronic disability that (1) is attributable to a mental or physical impairment or a combination of mental or physical impairments, (2) manifests before age 22, (3) is likely to continue indefinitely, and (4) results in substantial functional limitations in three or more major life activities.	Same.	Same.
Social Security Definition	No provision	Inability to engage in substantial gainful activity by reason of a physical or mental	No Provision

		impairment which can be expected to result in death or to last for not less than 12 months.	
HIV/AIDS Status	"A person infected with the human acquired immunodeficiency virus (HIV)" if they meet the definition of "person with disabilities" in the statute. "A person whose sole impairment is a diagnosis of HIV positive ... (i.e. does not meet the qualifying criteria in [the statute]) will not be eligible for occupancy in a Section 811 project."	The term person with disabilities "shall not exclude persons who have the disease of acquired immunodeficiency syndrome or any conditions arising from the etiologic agent..."	"Persons infected with the human acquired immunodeficiency virus (HIV) who are disabled as a result of infection with the HIV are eligible for occupancy in Section 202 projects ..."
Drug and/or Alcohol Addiction	"A person whose sole impairment is a diagnosis of ... alcoholism or drug addiction ... will not be eligible for occupancy in a Section 811 project."	Substantially the same.	Substantially the same.

Endnotes

[1] See, for example, Margery Austin Turner, Carla Herbig, Deborah Kaye, Julie Fenderson, and Diane Levy, *Discrimination Against Persons with Disabilities: Barriers at Every Step*, U.S. Department of Housing and Urban Development, May 2005, pp. 2-4, available at [http://www.huduser.org/Publications/pdf/DDS_Barriers.pdf].

[2] Claudia Center et al., "The Garrett History Brief," *Journal of Disability Policy Studies* 12, no. 2 (2001): 72-73 (hereafter "The Garrett History Brief").

[3] See, for example, O'Day, Bonnie, and Marcie Goldstein. "Advocacy Issues and Strategies for the 21st Century: Key Informant Interviews." *Journal of Disability Policy Studies* 15, no. 4 (January 1, 2005): 244.

[4] Laurie E. Powers, Jo-Ann Sowers, and George H. S. Singer, "A Cross-Disability Analysis of Person-Directed, Long-Term Services," *Journal of Disability Policy Studies* 17, no. 2 (January 1, 2006): 72.

[5] The Garrett History Brief, pp. 7 1-72.

[6] See, for example, Ann O'Hara, "HR 5772 — The Frank Melville Supportive Housing Investment Act of 2008 — Promotes Community Integration for People with Disabilities," Opening Doors, a Publication of the Technical Assistance Collaborative and the Consortium for Citizens with Disabilities Housing Task Force, May 2008, available at [http://www.tacinc.org/Docs/HH/OpeningDoors/ODIssue31.pdf].

[7] *Olmstead v. L.C.*, 527 U.S. 581, 607 (1999).

[8] Executive Order 13217, "Community-Based Alternatives for Individuals with Disabilities," *Federal Register*, vol. 66, no. 120, June 21, 2001, p. 33155.

[9] See, for example, Linda Velgouse and Molly Dworken, *Olmstead Update*, Presentation for the American Association of Homes and Services for the Aging Annual Meeting, October 2002.

[10] The Fair Housing Act is codified at Title 42, Chapter 45 of the United States Code. See sections 3601-3619. For more information about the Fair Housing Act, see CRS Report 95-710, *The Fair Housing Act: A Legal Overview*, by David H. Carpenter.

[11] 42 U.S.C. §3602(h).

[12] 42 U.S.C. §3604(f)(3)(C).

[13] 42 U.S.C. §3604(f)(3)(A).

[14] 42 U.S.C. §3604(f)(3)(B).

[15] Examples of reasonable modifications are also in regulation. See 24 C.F.R. § 100.203.

[16] See *Reasonable Modifications Under the Fair Housing Act*, Joint Statement of The Department of Housing and Urban Development and the Department of Justice, March 5, 2008, p. 4, available at [http://www.hud.gov/offices/fheo/disabilities/reasonable_ modifications_ mar08.pdf].

[17] Ibid., p. 3.

[18] 24 CFR § 100.203(a).

[19] Terry Moore and Beth O'Connell, *Compendium of Home Modification and Assistive Technology Policy and Practice Across the States*, Abt Associates, prepared for the U.S. Department of Health and Human Services, October 27, 2006, available at [http://www.hcbs.org/files/138/6854/assistive_tech_final_report.pdf].

[20] See *Reasonable Accommodations Under the Fair Housing Act*, Joint Statement of the Department of Housing and Urban Development and the Department of Justice, May 17, 2004, available at [http://www.nhl.gov/offices/fheo/library/huddoj statement.pdf].

[21] Ibid., pp. 8-9.

[22] 42 U.S.C. §8013(b).

[23] Although other terms may be preferred, this report uses the term "elderly" to refer to those individuals eligible for HUD-assisted housing for persons age 62 or older because it is the term used by HUD.

[24] For more information about the Section 202 program, see CRS Report RL33508, *Section 202 and Other HUD Rental Housing Programs for Low-Income Elderly Residents*, by Libby Perl.

[25] U.S. Department of Housing and Urban Development, *Housing for the Elderly and Handicapped: The Experience of the Section 202 Program from 1959 to 1977*, January 1979, p. 36 (hereafter *Housing for the Elderly and Handicapped*).

[26] Ibid., p. 67.

[27] See Section 210 of P.L. 93-383. "A person shall also be considered handicapped if such person is a developmentally disabled individual as defined in section 102(5) of the Developmental Disabilities Services and Facilities Construction Amendments of 1950."

[28] See discussion in U.S. Department of Housing and Urban Development, *Standards and Criteria for Housing for the Chronically Mentally Ill in the Section 202/8 Direct Loan Program*, April 1983, pp. 1-3 (hereafter *Standards and Criteria for Housing for the Chronically Mentally Ill*).

[29] Conference Report to accompany S. 3084, The Housing and Community Development Amendments of 1978, 95th Cong., 2nd sess., H.Rept. 95-1792.

[30] *Standards and Criteria for Housing for the Chronically Mentally Ill*, p. 2.

[31] See U.S. Department of Housing and Urban Development, "Section 202 Loans for Housing for the Elderly or Handicapped; Announcement of

Fund Availability, FY1982," *Federal Register*, vol. 47, no. 76, April 20, 1982, pp. 16892-16894.

[32] Housing provided for persons with disabilities through the Section 202 program is sometimes referred to as "Section 202(h)" housing, referring to the subparagraph that was added to the Section 202 statute by P.L. 95-557.

[33] See Senate Committee on Banking, Housing, and Urban Affairs, S.Rept. 95-871, Senate report to accompany S. 3084, the Housing and Community Development Act of 1977, 95th Cong., 2nd sess., May 15, 1978. The Senate bill became the Housing and Community Development Amendments of 1978 (P.L. 95-557).

[34] *Housing for the Elderly and Handicapped*, pp. 16-17.

[35] U.S. Department of Housing and Urban Development, FY1980 Budget Justifications, p. K-3.

[36] See H.Rept. 95-1161, House Committee on Banking, Finance, and Urban Affairs Report to accompany H.R. 12433, The Housing and Community Development Amendments of 1978, 95th Cong., 2nd sess. Portions of H.R. 12433 were inserted in the Senate version of the Housing and Community Development Amendments (S. 3084) which was enacted as P.L. 95-557.

[37] House Committee on Aging, Subcommittee on Housing and Consumer Interests, *The 1988 National Survey of Section 202 Housing for the Elderly and Handicapped*, 10 1st Cong., 1st sess., December 1, 1989, p. 99.

[38] U.S. Department of Housing and Urban Development, *Evaluation of Supportive Housing Programs for Persons with Disabilities*, July 1995, p. 8, available at [http://www.huduser.org/Publications/pdf/suphous1.pdf].

[39] See H.Rept. 100-498, Conference Report to accompany H.J.Res. 395, a joint resolution making continuing appropriations for FY1988; P.L. 100-404, the FY1989 HUD Appropriations Act; P.L. 101-144, the FY1 990 HUD Appropriations Act; and P.L. 101-507, the FY 1991 HUD Appropriations Act.

[40] House Committee on Banking, Finance, and Urban Affairs, H.Rept. 100-122, to accompany H.R. 4, the Housing, Community Development, and Homeless Prevention Act of 1987, 1 10th Cong., 1st sess., June 2, 1987.

[41] See Section 162 of P.L. 100-242.

[42] The Section 202 units funded with this new rental assistance are sometimes called "Section 202/162 PACs," referring to the section of the Housing

and Community Development Act of 1987, as well as the new "project assistance contracts" created by P.L. 100-242.

[43] S.Rept. 101-316, Report of the Senate Committee on Banking, Housing, and Urban Affairs, to accompany S. 566, the National Affordable Housing Act, 101st Cong., 2nd sess., June 8, 1990, p. 148.

[44] Ibid.

[45] 42 U.S.C. §8013(k)(2).

[46] Ibid.

[47] 42 U.S.C. § 15002(8).

[48] 24 C.F.R. §891.305.

[49] HUD funds housing specifically for persons living with HIV/AIDS through the Housing Opportunities for Persons with AIDS (HOPWA) program. For more information about HOPWA, see CRS Report RL343 18, *Housing Opportunities for Persons with AIDS (HOP WA)* , by Libby Perl.

[50] The definition of person with disabilities for the Section 8 and Public Housing programs is at 42 U.S.C. §1437a(b)(3) and 24 C.F.R. §5.403.

[51] 24 C.F.R. §891.505.

[52] See 42 U.S.C. §423(d).

[53] For a more detailed discussion of the Social Security Act definition of "disability" see CRS Report RL3 2279, *Primer on Disability Benefits: Social Security Disability Insurance (SSDI) and Supplemental Security Income (SSI)*, by Scott Szymendera.

[54] Non-elderly persons with disabilities do not reside in Section 202 developments funded through capital grants.

[55] U.S. Department of Housing and Urban Development, "FY2008 SuperNOFA for HUD's Discretionary Programs," *Federal Register*, vol. 73, no. 92, May 12, 2008, p. 27320. The NOFA is available on the HUD website with different pagination at [http://www.hud.gov/offices/adm/grants/nofa08/8 11 sec.pdf] (hereafter "FY2008 HUD NOFA").

[56] 42 U.S.C. §8013(e)(1).

[57] U.S. Department of Housing and Urban Development, *FY2007 Performance and Accountability Report*, November 15, 2007, p. 439, available at [http://www.hud.gov/offices/cfo/reports/2007/2007par.pdf].

[58] 42 U.S.C. §8013(c)(1).

[59] FY2008 HUD NOFA, p. 27325.

[60] Ibid.

[61] 24 C.F.R. §891.3 10.

[62] FY2008 HUD NOFA, p. 27325.

[63] 42 U.S.C. §8013(k)(1).

[64] 42 U.S.C. §8013(k)(4).

[65] FY2008 HUD NOFA p. 27325. Project sponsors may request an exception to the project size limitation if they can show site control.

[66] Ibid.

[67] Ibid., pp. 27325-27326.

[68] Ibid., p. 27319.

[69] Ibid.

[70] Ibid., p. 27332.

[71] 42 U.S.C. §8013(d)(2).

[72] 42 U.S.C. §8013(d).

[73] 42 U.S.C. §8013(d)(3).

[74] 42 U.S.C. §8013(k)(3).

[75] FY2008 HUD NOFA, p. 27334.

[76] Ibid.

[77] FY2008 HUD NOFA, pp. 27332-27333.

[78] For example, HUD's Shelter Plus Care and Supportive Housing Programs make tenant- based rental assistance available for homeless individuals. For more information about these programs see CRS Report RL33764, *The HUD Homeless Assistance Grants: Distribution of Funds*, by Libby Perl.

[79] 42 U.S.C. §8103(d)(4).

[80] U.S. Department of Housing and Urban Development, "Mainstream Housing Opportunities for Persons with Disabilities FY1999 Funding Availability," *Federal Register*, vol. 64, no. 44, March 8, 1999, p. 11303.

[81] For more information on criteria used to select applicants, see, for example, U.S. Department of Housing and Urban Development, "Notice of Funding Availability for FY2005 Mainstream Housing Opportunities for Persons with Disabilities Program," *Federal Register*, vol. 70, no. 211, November 2, 2005, pp. 66730-66732.

[82] See Department of Housing and Urban Development Notice PIH-2005-5, "New Freedom Initiative, Executive Order 13217: 'Community-Based Alternatives for Individuals with Disabilities,' and the Housing Choice Voucher Program," February 1, 2005, available at [http://www.hud.gov/offices/adm/hudclips/notices/pih/files/05-5PIHN.doc] (hereafter, "HUD Notice PIH-

2005-5"). PIH-2005-5 was extended indefinitely by PIH Letter L-2007-01, available at [http://www.hud.gov/offices/adm/hudclips/letters/07-1PIHL.doc].

[83] See, for example, the Consortium for Citizens with Disabilities, Letter to Josh B. Bolton, Director of the Office of Management and Budget, January 14, 2005. "[T]he CCD Housing Task Force believes there is a high likelihood that at least some of these precious 811 tenant based funds are being used to support non-disabled households."

[84] The first appropriations act to have this requirement was the FY2005 Consolidated Appropriations Act, P.L. 108-447.

[85] In a notice dated August 5, 2004, HUD noted that mainstream vouchers would be tracked in its data set. See Notice PIH-2004-13, "Codes for Special Programs Reported on the Family Report," available at [http:// www.hud.gov/offices/adm/hudclips/notices/pih/files/ 04-1 3PIHN.doc].

[86] *HUD FY2007 Performance and Accountability Report*, p. 439.

[87] Tenants with disabilities may also live in assisted housing units that are not specifically designated for their use.

[88] Prior to this, HUD's definition of elderly families did not include single individuals.

[89] Frances Merchant Carp, *A Future for the Aged, Victoria Plaza and Its Residents* (Austin: University of Texas Press, 1966).

[90] The Housing Act of 1961 (P.L. 87-70) made all households in which an adult member has a disability eligible for public housing. Prior to this, in the Housing Act of 1959 (P.L. 86- 372), near-elderly households with an adult member with a disability were made eligible. Near-elderly households are those with an adult member age 50 and older.

[91] See General Accounting Office (now the Government Accountability Office), *Housing Persons with Mental Disabilities with the Elderly*, GAO/RCED-92-8 1, August 1992, pp. 10- 11, available at [http://archive. gao.gov/d33t1 0/147294.pdf].

[92] According to the House Judiciary Committee Report accompanying H.R. 1158, the Fair Housing Act Amendments of 1988, enacted as P.L. 100-430, the bill used the same definitions and concepts from the Rehabilitation Act of 1973 (P.L. 93-112), which included drug addiction and alcoholism as physical or mental impairments (see 28 CFR §41.31). However, under P.L. 100-430, handicap does not include "current, illegal use of or addiction to a controlled substance."

[93] *Housing Persons with Mental Disabilities with the Elderly*, p. 17. See, also, remarks of Representative Peter Blute, *Congressional Record*, daily edition, vol. 142 (February 27, 1996), p. H1274.

[94] The provisions are codified at 42 U.S.C. §1437e; the regulations are at 24 CFR §§945.101-945.303.

[95] HUD Designated Housing Status Report, available at [http://www.hud.gov/offices/pih/ programs/ph/dhp/designated.cfm].

[96] The new construction and substantial rehabilitation program was created in P.L. 93-383; authority to enter into new contracts was suspended in P.L. 98-181. For more information on Section 8 housing, see CRS Report RL32284, *An Overview of the Section 8 Program*, by Maggie McCarty.

[97] The provisions are codified at 42 U.S.C. §§1361 1-13620.

[98] 42 U.S.C. §1437a(b)(3).

[99] Specifically, the statute refers to the higher of the number of units occupied by individuals or families with disabilities on either October 28, 1992 or January 1, 1992. 42 U.S.C. § 13612(b).

[100] 42 U.S.C. §13613.

[101] This 40% cap on a tenant's contribution is in effect only for the first year. After the first year, if rent increases and the family wishes to continue to live in the unit, then the family can choose to contribute more than 40% of its income toward rent.

[102] For more information about the Section 8 program, see CRS Report RL32284, *An Overview of the Section 8 Housing Programs*, by Maggie McCarty.

[103] See Title VI, Subtitle B of P.L. 102-5 50 for Public Housing and Title VI, Subtitle D for Section 8. The law also gave authority to owners of Section 202, Section 221(d)(3), and Section 236 properties to continue to restrict occupancy to elderly families according to the rules in place at the time the projects were developed (see Section 658).

[104] Amounts appropriated from FY1997 through FY2002 were $50 million in FY1997 (P.L. 104-204) and $40 million in each of FY1998 (P.L. 105-65), FY1999 (P.L. 105-276), FY2000 (P.L. 106-74), FY2001 (P.L. 106-377), and FY2002 (P.L. 107-73).

[105] The phrase "to the extent practicable" appeared in appropriations laws beginning in FY2003 (P.L. 108-7) through FY2006 (P.L. 109-115). The FY2007 House-passed HUD appropriations bill (H.R. 5576) also contained this phrase, but a year-long continuing resolution was enacted in

lieu of separate appropriations laws. The FY2008 HUD Appropriations Act did not contain this phrase.

[106] HUD Notice PIH-2005-5.

[107] For more background on the evolution of federal housing assistance policy, see CRS Report RL3459 1, *Overview of Federal Housing Assistance Programs and Policy*, by Maggie McCarty, Libby Perl, Bruce Foote, and Meredith Peterson.

[108] For more information on the LIHTC, see CRS Report RS22389, *An Introduction to the Design of the Low-Income Housing Tax Credit*, by Mark P. Keightley.

[109] 26 U.S.C. §42(g).

[110] 26 U.S.C. §42(m)(1)(B).

[111] Until enactment of P.L. 110-289, the Housing and Economic Recovery Act of 2008, the LIHTC statute contained eight selection criteria. P.L. 110-289 added two more. See 26 U.S.C. §42(m)(1)(C).

[112] See Joseph Guggenheim, *Tax Credits for Low Income Housing* (Glen Echo, MD: Simon Publications, 1996) p. 33.

[113] For more information about how state QAPs promote housing for populations with special needs, see James Tassos, *Housing Credit Policies in 2007 That Promote Supportive Housing*, The Corporation for Supportive Housing and Enterprise Community Partners, available at http: //www.practitionerresources.org/cache/documents/657/65721 .pdf]. The report was updated with an addendum for 2008. That report is available at [http://documents.csh.org/documents/pubs/QAP Study2008Update.pdf].

[114] *Housing Credit Policies in 2007 That Promote Supportive Housing*, p. 9.

[115] Ibid., p. 10.

[116] Ibid., p. 13.

[117] The HOME program is codified at 42 U.S.C. §§12741-12756.

[118] 24 C.F.R. §92.50(c). In general, in order to be considered a "participating jurisdiction" eligible for HOME funds, a locality must qualify for at least $750,000 under the HOME formula. 42 U.S.C. § 12746. All states receive allocations under the HOME formula. 42 U.S.C. §12747(b)(2).

[119] The other three programs are the Community Development Block Grant, Housing Opportunities for Persons with AIDS, and the Emergency Shelter Grants.

[120] 24 C.F.R. §91.205 and §91.305.

[121] 24 C.F.R. §91.105 and §91.115.

[122] 24 C.F.R. §91.110.

[123] 24 C.F.R. §91.215 and §92.209.

[124] 24 C.F.R. §92.209(c)(2).

[125] 24 C.F.R.§92.2.

[126] 42 U.S.C. §5301(c).

[127] 42 U.S.C. §5306.

[128] Ibid.

[129] HUD Notice CPD-050-03, "Implementing the New Freedom Initiative and Involving Persons with Disabilities in the Preparation of the Consolidated Plan through Citizen Participation," June 6, 2005, available at [http://www.hud.gov/offices/adm/hudclips/notices/ cpd/05-3c.doc].

[130] 42 U.S.C. §5305(a)(5).

[131] HUD Notice CPD-050-03.

[132] Specifically, a property's qualified basis is determined as follows: (1) the cost of constructing, acquiring, or rehabilitating the property is calculated, (2) this amount is reduced by federal grants received by the developer, and (3) the resulting value is then multiplied by the percentage of space in the housing development that is devoted to low- income use. This percentage is the lower of either the "unit fraction" — the ratio of low-income units to all units in the building — or the "floor space fraction" — the ratio of square footage in low-income units to total square footage. 26 U.S.C. §42(c). The qualified basis is then multiplied by the value of the tax credits — these are roughly either 9% or 4% — to determine the total annual value of the tax credits.

[133] In addition to the costs of materials, construction, and/or rehabilitation, among the costs included in determining qualified basis are: contractor fees, developer fees, engineering fees and the cost of drawing up architectural specifications. Among the costs that are not included are the cost of land and fees associated with long-term financing. See Joseph Guggenheim, *Tax Credits for Low Income Housing* (Glen Echo, MD: Simon Publications, 1996) p. 37.

[134] See HUD website, "Calculating the Qualified Basis," available at [http://www.hud.gov/offices/cpd/affordablehousing/training/web/lihtc/calculating/qualifi edbasis.cfm].

[135] 26 C.F.R. § 1.42-16.

[136] Rev. Rul. 2008-6.

[137] Rev. Rul. 2002-65.

[138] Rev. Rul. 98-49.

[139] P.L. 106-569 amended the Section 811 statute to state that "[n]otwithstanding any other provision of law, assistance amounts provided under this section may be treated as amounts not derived from a Federal grant." See Section 842. On September 17, 2003, the IRS issued a letter stating that it was reviewing the applicability of the LIHTC section of federal grants to PRAC under the Section 202 program. The letter is available at [http://www.irs.gov/ pub/irs-wd/04-006 1 .pdf].

[140] These credit rates are not set exactly at 9% and 4% — they vary depending on the current interest rate used in the Department of the Treasury credit rate formula. For more information about this issue, see CRS Report RS229 17, *The Low-Income Housing Tax Credit Program: The Fixed Subsidy and Variable Rate*, by Mark P. Keightley.

[141] The statute also specifically exempted funds received under CDBG, HOME, and Native American Housing and Self Determination Act programs from the definition of federally subsidized, so those projects have been eligible for the 9% credit all along.

[142] See U.S. Department of Housing and Urban Development, "Mixed Finance Development for Supportive Housing for the Elderly or Persons with Disabilities: Final Rule," *Federal Register* vol. 70, no. 176, September 13, 2005, p. 54202.

[143] See, for example, Liz Enochs, "Affordable Housing Equity: Developers Share Tips for Converting Projects That Fail to Win 9% LIHTCs into 4% Deals," *Affordable Housing Finance*, July 2007, available at [http://www. housingfinance.com/ahf/articles/2007/jul/ AFFORDABLE0707.htm].

[144] For the most recent report see U.S. Department of Housing and Urban Development, *Affordable Housing Needs 2005*, May 2007, available at [http://www.huduser.org/ Publications/pdf/AffHsgNeeds.pdf] (hereafter *Affordable Housing Needs 2005*).

[145] HUD developed the definition using preference rules for admission to assisted housing. See *Affordable Housing Needs 2005*, p. 7.

[146] For more information see *Affordable Housing Needs 2005*, pp. 85-86.

[147] Ibid., p. 13.

[148] Ibid., p. 19.

[149] U.S. Department of Housing and Urban Development, *Housing Needs of Persons with Disabilities: Supplemental Findings to the Affordable Housing Needs 2005 Report*, February 2008, available at [http://www.

huduser.org/Publications/pdf/Affhsgneedsdis.pdf] (hereafter *Supplemental Findings to the Affordable Housing Needs 2005 Report*).

[150] Ibid., pp. 1-2.

[151] Kathryn P. Nelson, *The Hidden Housing Crisis: Worst Case Housing Needs Among Adults with Disabilities*, Consortium for Citizens with Disabilities Housing Task Force, March 2008, available at [http://www.tacinc.org/Docs/HH/HiddenHousingCrisis.pdf].

[152] Ibid.

[153] Peter H. Rossi, *Down and Out in America: The Origins of Homelessness* (Chicago: The University of Chicago Press, 1989), p. 33.

[154] Ibid., pp. 181-194, 41. See, also, Martha Burt, *Over the Edge: The Growth of Homelessness in the 1980s* (New York: Russell Sage Foundation, 1992), pp. 31-126.

[155] See Randall Kuhn and Dennis P. Culhane, "Applying Cluster Analysis to Test a Typology of Homelessness by Pattern of Shelter Utilization: Results from the Analysis of Administrative Data," *American Journal of Community Psychology* 26, no. 2 (April 1998): 210-212.

[156] 24 C.F.R. §9 1.5.

[157] U.S. Department of Housing and Urban Development, *The Third Annual Homeless Assessment Report to Congress*, July 2008, p. 16, available at [http://www.hudhre.info/ documents/3rdHomelessAssessmentReport.pdf]; Carol L. M. Caton, Carol Wilkins, and Jacquelyn Anderson, *People Who Experience Long-Term Homelessness: Characteristics and Intervention*, 2007 National Symposium on Homelessness Research, September 2007, p. 4-3, available at [http://www.huduser.org/publications/pdf/p4.pdf] (hereafter *People Who Experience Long-Term Homelessness: Characteristics and Intervention*).

[158] *People Who Experience Long-Term Homelessness: Characteristics and Intervention*, p. 4-4.

[159] See, for example, D.P. Culhane, E. Gollub, R. Kuhn, and M. Shpaner, "The Co- Occurrence of AIDS and Homelessness: Results from the Integration of Administrative Databases for AIDS Surveillance, and Public Shelter Utilization in Philadelphia," *Journal of Epidemiology and Community Health* 55, no. 7 (2001): 515-520. Marjorie Robertson, et al., "HIV Seroprevalence Among Homeless and Marginally Housed Adults in San Francisco," *American Journal of Public Health* 94, no. 7 (2004): 1207-1217. Angela A. Aidala and Gunj eong Lee, *Housing Services and*

Housing Stability Among Persons Living with HIV/AIDS, Joseph L. Mailman School of Public Health, May 30, 2000, available online at [http://www.nyhiv.org/pdfs/chain/ CHAIN%20Housing%20Stability%2032.pdf].

160 For more information about these grants, see CRS Report RL33764, *The HUD Homeless Assistance Grants: Distribution of Funds*, by Libby Perl.

161 *People Who Experience Long-Term Homelessness: Characteristics and Intervention*, p. 4-23.

162 See, for example, Written Statement of Ann O'Hara, Consortium for Citizens with Disabilities Housing Task Force, for the hearing before the House Financial Services Committee, Subcommittee on Housing and Community Opportunity, *H.R. 5772, The Frank Melville Supportive Housing Investment Act of 2008*, 110th Cong., 2nd sess., June 20, 2008, available at [http://www.house.gov/apps/list/hearing/financialsvcs_dem/ o'hara062008.pdf].

In: HUD Housing Programs for Persons ... ISBN 978-1-60741-113-0
Editor: Ervin C. Felker, pp. 51-75

Chapter 2

JOINT STATEMENT OF THE DEPARTMENT OF HOUSING AND URBAN DEVELOPMENT AND THE DEPARTMENT OF JUSTICE. REASONABLE MODIFICATIONS UNDER THE FAIR HOUSING ACT*

U.S. Department of Justice
Civil Rights Division
U.S. Department of Housing and Urban Development Office
of Fair Housing and Equal Opportunity

INTRODUCTION

The Department of Justice ("DOJ") and the Department of Housing and Urban Development ("HUD") are jointly responsible for enforcing the federal Fair Housing Act[1] (the "Act"), which prohibits discrimination in housing on the basis of race, color, religion, sex, national origin, familial status, and

* This is an edited, excerpted and augmented edition of a U.S. Department of Justice and U.S. Department of Housing and Urban Development publication, Washington D.C., dated March 5, 2008.

disability.[2] One type of disability discrimination prohibited by the Act is a refusal to permit, at the expense of the person with a disability, reasonable modifications of existing premises occupied or to be occupied by such person if such modifications may be necessary to afford such person full enjoyment of the premises.[3] HUD and DOJ frequently respond to complaints alleging that housing providers have violated the Act by refusing reasonable modifications to persons with disabilities. This Statement provides technical assistance regarding the rights and obligations of persons with disabilities and housing providers under the Act relating to reasonable modifications.[4]

This Statement is not intended to provide specific guidance regarding the Act's design and construction requirements for multifamily dwellings built for first occupancy after March 13, 1991. Some of the reasonable modifications discussed in this Statement are features of accessible design that are required for covered multifamily dwellings pursuant to the Act's design and construction requirements. As a result, people involved in the design and construction of multifamily dwellings are advised to consult the Act at 42 U.S.C. § 3604(f)(3)(c), the implementing regulations at 24 C.F.R. § 100.205, the Fair Housing Accessibility Guidelines, and the Fair Housing Act Design Manual. All of these are available on HUD's website at www.hud.gov/offices/fheo/disabilities/index.cfm. Additional technical guidance on the design and construction requirements can also be found on HUD's website and the Fair Housing Accessibility FIRST website at: http://www.fairhousingfirst.org.

QUESTIONS AND ANSWERS

1. What Types of Discrimination against Persons with Disabilities does the Act Prohibit?

The Act prohibits housing providers from discriminating against housing applicants or residents because of their disability or the disability of anyone associated with them and from treating persons with disabilities less favorably than others because of their disability. The Act makes it unlawful for any person to refuse "to permit, at the expense of the [disabled] person, reasonable modifications of existing premises occupied or to be occupied by such person if such modifications may be necessary to afford such person full enjoyment of the premises, except that, in the case of a rental, the landlord may where it is reasonable to do so condition permission for a modification on the renter agreeing to restore the interior of the premises to the condition that existed before the modification, reasonable wear and tear excepted."[5] The Act also makes it unlawful for any person to refuse "to make reasonable accommodations in rules, policies, practices, or services, when such accommodations may be necessary to afford ... person(s) [with disabilities] equal opportunity to use and enjoy a dwelling." The Act also prohibits housing providers from refusing residency to persons with disabilities, or, with some narrow exceptions[6], placing conditions on their residency, because those persons may require reasonable modifications or reasonable accommodations.

2. What Is a Reasonable Modification under the Fair Housing Act?

A reasonable modification is a structural change made to existing premises, occupied or to be occupied by a person with a disability, in order to afford such person full enjoyment of the premises. Reasonable modifications can include structural changes to interiors and exteriors of dwellings and to common and public use areas. A request for a reasonable modification may be made at any time during the tenancy. The Act makes it unlawful for a housing provider or homeowners' association to refuse to allow a reasonable modification to the premises when such a modification may be necessary to afford persons with disabilities full enjoyment of the premises.

To show that a requested modification may be necessary, there must be an identifiable relationship, or nexus, between the requested modification and the individual's disability. Further, the modification must be "reasonable." Examples of modifications that typically are reasonable include widening doorways to make rooms more accessible for persons in wheelchairs; installing grab bars in bathrooms; lowering kitchen cabinets to a height suitable for persons in wheelchairs; adding a ramp to make a primary entrance accessible for persons in wheelchairs; or altering a walkway to provide access to a public or common use area. These examples of reasonable modifications are not exhaustive.

3. Who is Responsible for the Expense of Making a Reasonable Modification?

The Fair Housing Act provides that while the housing provider must permit the modification, the tenant is responsible for paying the cost of the modification.

4. Who Qualifies as a Person with a Disability under the Act?

The Act defines a person with a disability to include (1) individuals with a physical or mental impairment that substantially limits one or more major life activities; (2) individuals who are regarded as having such an impairment; and (3) individuals with a record of such an impairment.

The term "physical or mental impairment" includes, but is not limited to, such diseases and conditions as orthopedic, visual, speech and hearing impairments, cerebral palsy, autism, epilepsy, muscular dystrophy, multiple sclerosis, cancer, heart disease, diabetes, Human Immunodeficiency Virus infection, mental retardation, emotional illness, drug addiction (other than addiction caused by current, illegal use of a controlled substance) and alcoholism.

The term "substantially limits" suggests that the limitation is "significant" or "to a large degree."

The term "major life activity" means those activities that are of central importance to daily life, such as seeing, hearing, walking, breathing, performing manual tasks, caring for one's self, learning, and speaking. This list of major life activities is not exhaustive.

5. Who is Entitled to a Reasonable Modification under the Fair Housing Act?

Persons who meet the Fair Housing Act's definition of "person with a disability" may be entitled to a reasonable modification under the Act. However, there must be an identifiable relationship, or nexus, between the requested modification and the individual's disability. If no such nexus exists, then the housing provider may refuse to allow the requested modification.

Example 1: A tenant, whose arthritis impairs the use of her hands and causes her substantial difficulty in using the doorknobs in her apartment, wishes to replace the doorknobs with levers. Since there is a relationship between the tenant's disability and the requested modification and the modification is reasonable, the housing provider must allow her to make the modification at the tenant's expense.

Example 2: A homeowner with a mobility disability asks the condo association to permit him to change his roofing from shaker shingles to clay tiles and fiberglass shingles because he alleges that the shingles are less fireproof and put him at greater risk during a fire. There is no evidence that the shingles permitted by the homeowner's association provide inadequate fire protection and the person with the disability has not identified a nexus between his disability and the need for clay tiles and fiberglass shingles. The homeowner's association is not required to permit the homeowner's modification because the homeowner's request is not reasonable and there is no nexus between the request and the disability.

6. If a Disability is not Obvious, what Kinds of Information May a Housing Provider Request from the Person with a Disability in Support of a Requested Reasonable Modification?

A housing provider may not ordinarily inquire as to the nature and severity of an individual's disability. However, in response to a request for a reasonable modification, a housing provider may request reliable disability-related information that (1) is necessary to verify that the person meets the Act's definition of disability (i.e., has a physical or mental impairment that substantially limits one or more major life activities), (2) describes the needed modification, and (3) shows the relationship between the person's disability and the need for the requested modification. Depending on the individual's circumstances, information verifying that the person meets the Act's definition of disability can usually be provided by the individual herself (e.g., proof that an individual under 65 years of age receives Supplemental Security Income or Social Security Disability Insurance benefits[7] or a credible statement by the individual). A doctor or other medical professional, a peer support group, a non-medical service agency, or a reliable third party who is in a position to know about the individual's disability may also provide verification of a disability. In most cases, an individual's medical records or detailed information about the nature of a person's disability is not necessary for this inquiry.

Once a housing provider has established that a person meets the Act's definition of disability, the provider's request for documentation should seek only the information that is necessary to evaluate if the reasonable modification is needed because of a disability. Such information must be kept confidential and must not be shared with other persons unless they need the information to make or assess a decision to grant or deny a reasonable modification request or unless disclosure is required by law (e.g., a court-issued subpoena requiring disclosure).

7. What Kinds of Information, if any, May a Housing Provider Request from a Person with an Obvious or Known Disability who is Requesting a Reasonable Modification?

A housing provider is entitled to obtain information that is necessary to evaluate whether a requested reasonable modification may be necessary because of a disability. If a person's disability is obvious, or otherwise known to the housing provider, and if the need for the requested modification is also readily apparent or known, then the provider may not request any additional information about the requester's disability or the disability-related need for the modification.

If the requester's disability is known or readily apparent to the provider, but the need for the modification is not readily apparent or known, the provider may request only information that is necessary to evaluate the disability-related need for the modification.

Example 1: An applicant with an obvious mobility impairment who uses a motorized scooter to move around asks the housing provider to permit her to install a ramp at the entrance of the apartment building. Since the physical disability (i.e., difficulty walking) and the disability-related need for the requested modification are both readily apparent, the provider may not require the applicant to provide any additional information about her disability or the need for the requested modification.

Example 2: A deaf tenant asks his housing provider to allow him to install extra electrical lines and a cable line so the tenant can use computer equipment that helps him communicate with others. If the tenant's disability is known, the housing provider may not require him to document his disability; however, since the need for the electrical and cable lines may not be apparent, the housing provider may request information that is necessary to support the disability-related need for the requested modification.

8. Who must Comply with the Fair Housing Act's Reasonable Modification Requirements?

Any person or entity engaging in prohibited conduct – i.e., refusing to allow an individual to make reasonable modifications when such modifications may be necessary to afford a person with a disability full enjoyment of the premises – may be held liable unless they fall within an exception to the Act's coverage. Courts have applied the Act to individuals, corporations, associations and others involved in the provision of housing and residential lending, including property owners, housing managers, homeowners and condominium associations, lenders, real estate agents, and brokerage services. Courts have also applied the Act to state and local governments, most often in the context of exclusionary zoning or other land-use decisions. See, e.g., City of Edmonds v. Oxford House, Inc., 514 U.S. 725, 729 (1995); Project Life v. Glendening, 139 F. Supp. 2d 703, 710 (D. Md. 2001), aff'd, 2002 WL 2012545 (4th Cir. 2002).

9. What is the Difference between a *Reasonable Accommodation* and a *Reasonable Modification* under the Fair Housing Act?[8]

Under the Fair Housing Act, a reasonable *modification* is a structural change made to the premises whereas a reasonable *accommodation* is a change, exception, or adjustment to a rule, policy, practice, or service. A person with a disability may need either a reasonable accommodation or a reasonable modification, or both, in order to have an equal opportunity to use and enjoy a dwelling, including public and common use spaces. Generally, under the Fair Housing Act, the housing provider is responsible for the costs associated with a reasonable accommodation unless it is an undue financial and administrative burden, while the tenant or someone acting on the tenant's behalf, is responsible for costs associated with a reasonable modification. See Reasonable Accommodation Statement, Questions 7 and 8.

Example 1: Because of a mobility disability, a tenant wants to install grab bars in the bathroom. This is a reasonable modification and must be permitted at the tenant's expense.

Example 2: Because of a hearing disability, a tenant wishes to install a peephole in her door so she can see who is at the door before she opens it. This is a reasonable modification and must be permitted at the tenant's expense.

Example 3: Because of a mobility disability, a tenant wants to install a ramp outside the building in a common area. This is a reasonable modification and must be permitted at the tenant's expense. See also Questions 19, 20 and 21.

Example 4: Because of a vision disability, a tenant requests permission to have a guide dog reside with her in her apartment. The housing provider has a "no-pets" policy. This is a request for a reasonable accommodation, and the housing provider must grant the accommodation.

10. Are Reasonable Modifications Restricted to the Interior of a Dwelling?

No. Reasonable modifications are not limited to the interior of a dwelling. Reasonable modifications may also be made to public and common use areas such as widening entrances to fitness centers or laundry rooms, or for changes to exteriors of dwelling units such as installing a ramp at the entrance to a dwelling.

11. Is a Request for a Parking Space because of a Physical Disability a *Reasonable Accommodation* or a *Reasonable Modification*?

Courts have treated requests for parking spaces as requests for a reasonable accommodation and have placed the responsibility for providing the parking space on the housing provider, even if provision of an accessible or assigned parking space results in some cost to the provider. For example, courts have required a housing provider to provide an assigned space even though the housing provider had a policy of not assigning parking spaces or had a waiting list for available parking. However, housing providers may not require persons with disabilities to pay extra fees as a condition of receiving accessible parking spaces.

Providing a parking accommodation could include creating signage, repainting markings, redistributing spaces, or creating curb cuts. This list is not exhaustive.

12. What if the Structural Changes being Requested by the Tenant or Applicant Are in a Building that is Subject to the Design and Construction Requirements of the Fair Housing Act and the Requested Structural Changes are a Feature of accessible Design that should have already Existed in the Unit or Common Area, *e.g.*, Doorways Wide enough to Accommodate a Wheelchair, or an Accessible Entryway to a Unit

The Fair Housing Act provides that covered multifamily dwellings built for first occupancy after March 13, 1991, shall be designed and constructed to meet certain minimum accessibility and adaptability standards. If any of the structural changes needed by the tenant are ones that should have been included in the unit or public and common use area when constructed then the housing provider may be responsible for providing and paying for those requested structural changes. However, if the requested structural changes are not a feature of accessible design that should have already existed in the building pursuant to the design and construction requirements under the Act, then the tenant is responsible for paying for the cost of the structural changes as a reasonable modification.

Although the design and construction provisions only apply to certain multifamily dwellings built for first occupancy since 1991, a tenant may request reasonable modifications to housing built prior to that date. In such cases, the housing provider must allow the modifications, and the tenant is responsible for paying for the costs under the Fair Housing Act.

For a discussion of the design and construction requirements of the Act, and their applicability, see HUD's website at: *www.hud.gov/offices/fheo/*

disabilities/index.cfm and the Fair Housing Accessibility FIRST website at: http://www.fairhousingfirst.org.

Example 1: A tenant with a disability who uses a wheelchair resides in a ground floor apartment in a non-elevator building that was built in 1995. Buildings built for first occupancy after March 13, 1991 are covered by the design and construction requirements of the Fair Housing Act. Because the building is a non-elevator building, all ground floor units must meet the minimum accessibility requirements of the Act. The doors in the apartment are not wide enough for passage using a wheelchair in violation of the design and construction requirements but can be made so through retrofitting. Under these circumstances, one federal court has held that the tenant may have a potential claim against the housing provider.

Example 2: A tenant with a disability resides in an apartment in a building that was built in 1987. The doors in the unit are not wide enough for passage using a wheelchair but can be made so through retrofitting. If the tenant meets the other requirements for obtaining a modification, the tenant may widen the doorways, at her own expense.

Example 3: A tenant with a disability resides in an apartment in a building that was built in 1993 in compliance with the design and construction requirements of the Fair Housing Act. The tenant wants to install grab bars in the bathroom because of her disability. Provided that the tenant meets the other requirements for obtaining a modification, the tenant may install the grab bars at her own expense.

13. Who is Responsible for Expenses Associated with a Reasonable Modification, e.g., for Upkeep or Maintenance?

The tenant is responsible for upkeep and maintenance of a modification that is used exclusively by her. If a modification is made to a common area that is normally maintained by the housing provider, then the housing provider is responsible for the upkeep and maintenance of the modification. If a modification is made to a common area that is not normally maintained by the housing provider, then the housing provider has no responsibility under the Fair Housing Act to maintain the modification.

Example 1: Because of a mobility disability, a tenant, at her own expense, installs a lift inside her unit to allow her access to a second story. She is required to maintain the lift at her expense because it is not in a common area.

Example 2: Because of a mobility disability, a tenant installs a ramp in the lobby of a multifamily building at her own expense. The ramp is used by other tenants and the public as well as the tenant with the disability. The housing provider is responsible for maintaining the ramp.

Example 3: A tenant leases a detached, single-family home. Because of a mobility disability, the tenant installs a ramp at the outside entrance to the home. The housing provider provides no snow removal services, and the lease agreement specifically states that snow removal is the responsibility of the individual tenant. Under these circumstances, the housing provider has no responsibility under the Fair Housing Act to remove snow on the tenant's ramp. However, if the housing provider normally provides snow removal for the outside of the building and the common areas, the housing provider is responsible for removing the snow from the ramp as well.

14. In Addition to Current Residents, Are Prospective Tenants and Buyers of Housing Protected by the Reasonable Modification Provisions of the Fair Housing Act?

Yes. A person may make a request for a reasonable modification at any time. An individual may request a reasonable modification of the dwelling at the time that the potential tenancy or purchase is discussed. Under the Act, a housing provider cannot deny or restrict access to housing because a request for a reasonable modification is made. Such conduct would constitute discrimination. The modification does not have to be made, however, unless it is reasonable. See Questions 2, 16, 21 and 23.

15. When and how should an Individual Request Permission to Make a Modification?

Under the Act, a resident or an applicant for housing makes a reasonable modification request whenever she makes clear to the housing provider that she is requesting permission to make a structural change to the premises because of her disability. She should explain that she has a disability, if not readily apparent or not known to the housing provider, the type of modification she is requesting, and the relationship between the requested modification and her disability.

An applicant or resident is not entitled to receive a reasonable modification unless she requests one. However, the Fair Housing Act does not require that a request be made in a particular manner or at a particular time. A person with a disability need not personally make the reasonable modification request; the request can be made by a family member or someone else who is acting on her behalf. An individual making a reasonable modification request does not need to mention the Act or use the words "reasonable modification." However, the requester must make the request in a manner that a reasonable person would understand to be a request for permission to make a structural change because of a disability.

Although a reasonable modification request can be made orally or in writing, it is usually helpful for both the resident and the housing provider if the request is made in writing. This will help prevent misunderstandings regarding what is being requested, or whether the request was made. To facilitate the processing and consideration of the request, residents or prospective residents may wish to check with a housing provider in advance to determine if the provider has a preference regarding the manner in which the request is made. However, housing providers must give appropriate consideration to reasonable modification requests even if the requester makes the request orally or does not use the provider's preferred forms or procedures for making such requests.

16. Does a Person with a Disability Have to Have the Housing Provider's Approval before Making a Reasonable Modification to the Dwelling?

Yes. A person with a disability must have the housing provider's approval before making the modification. However, if the person with a disability meets the requirements under the Act for a reasonable modification and provides the relevant documents and assurances, the housing provider cannot deny the request.

17. What if the Housing Provider Fails to Act Promptly on a Reasonable Modification Request?

A provider has an obligation to provide prompt responses to a reasonable modification request. An undue delay in responding to a reasonable modification request may be deemed a failure to permit a reasonable modification.

18. What if the Housing Provider Proposes that the Tenant Move to a Different Unit in lieu of Making a Proposed Modification?

The housing provider cannot insist that a tenant move to a different unit in lieu of allowing the tenant to make a modification that complies with the requirements for reasonable modifications. See Questions 2, 21 and 23. Housing providers should be aware that persons with disabilities typically have the most accurate knowledge regarding the functional limitations posed by their disability.

Example: As a result of a mobility disability, a tenant requests that he be permitted, at his expense, to install a ramp so that he can access his apartment using his motorized wheelchair. The existing entrance to his dwelling is not wheelchair accessible because the route to the front door requires going up a step. The housing provider proposes that in lieu of installing the ramp, the tenant move to a different unit in the building. The tenant is not obligated to accept the alternative proposed by the housing provider, as his request to modify his unit is reasonable and must be approved.

19. What if the Housing Provider Wants an Alternative Modification or Alternative Design for the Proposed Modification that does not Cost More but that the Housing Provider Considers more Aesthetically Pleasing?

In general, the housing provider cannot insist on an alternative modification or an alternative design if the tenant complies with the requirements for reasonable modifications. See Questions 2, 21 and 23. If the modification is to the interior of the unit and must be restored to its original condition when the tenant moves out, then the housing provider cannot require that its design be used instead of the tenant's design. However, if the modification is to a common area or an aspect of the interior of the unit that would not have to be restored because it would not be reasonable to do so, and if the housing provider's proposed design imposes no additional costs and still meets the tenant's needs, then the modification should be done in accordance with the housing provider's design. See Question 24 for a discussion of the restoration requirements.

Example 1: As a result of a mobility disability, a tenant requests that he be permitted, at his expense, to install a ramp so that he can access his apartment using his motorized wheelchair. The existing entrance to his dwelling is not wheelchair accessible because the route to the front door requires going up a step. The housing provider proposes an alternative design for a ramp but the alternative design costs more and does not meet the tenant's needs. The tenant is not obligated to accept the alternative modification, as his request to modify his unit is reasonable and must be approved.

Example 2: As a result of a mobility disability, a tenant requests permission to widen a doorway to allow passage with her wheelchair. All of the doorways in the unit are trimmed with a decorative trim molding that does not cost any more than the standard trim molding. Because in usual circumstances it would not be reasonable to require that the doorway be restored at the end of the tenancy, the tenant should use the decorative trim when he widens the doorway.

20. What if the Housing Provider Wants a more Costly Design for the Requested Modification?

If the housing provider wishes a modification to be made with more costly materials, in order to satisfy the landlord's aesthetic standards, the tenant must agree only if the housing provider pays those additional costs. Further, as discussed in Questions 21 and 23 below, housing providers may require that the tenant obtain all necessary building permits and may require that the work be performed in a workmanlike manner. If the housing provider requires more costly materials be used to satisfy her workmanship preferences beyond the requirements of the applicable local codes, the tenant must agree only if the housing provider pays for those additional costs as well. In such a case, however, the housing provider's design must still meet the tenant's needs.

21. What Types of Documents and Assurances May a Housing Provider Require Regarding the Modification before Granting the Reasonable Modification?

A housing provider may require that a request for a reasonable modification include a description of the proposed modification both before changes are made to the dwelling and before granting the modification. A description of the modification to be made may be provided to a housing provider either orally or in writing depending on the extent and nature of the proposed modification. A housing provider may also require that the tenant obtain any building permits needed to make the modifications, and that the work be performed in a workmanlike manner.

The regulations implementing the Fair Housing Act state that housing providers generally cannot impose conditions on a proposed reasonable modification. For example, a housing provider cannot require that the tenant obtain additional insurance or increase the security deposit as a condition that must be met before the modification will be allowed.

However, the Preamble to the Final Regulations also indicates that there are some conditions that can be placed on a tenant requesting a reasonable modification. For example, in certain limited and narrow circumstances, a housing provider may require that the tenant deposit money into an interest bearing account to ensure that funds are available to restore the interior of a dwelling to its previous state, ordinary wear and tear excepted. Imposing conditions not contemplated by the Fair Housing Act and its implementing regulations may be the same as an illegal refusal to permit the modification.

22. May a Housing Provider or Homeowner's Association Condition Approval of the Requested Modification on the Requester Obtaining Special liabiLity Insurance?

No. Imposition of such a requirement would constitute a violation of the Fair Housing Act.

Example: Because of a mobility disability, a tenant wants to install a ramp outside his unit. The housing provider informs the tenant that the ramp may be installed, but only after the tenant obtains separate liability insurance for the ramp out of concern for the housing provider's potential liability. The housing provider may not impose a requirement of liability insurance as a condition of approval of the ramp.

23. Once the Housing Provider has Agreed to a Reasonable Modification, may she Insist that a Particular Contractor be Used to Perform the Work?

No. The housing provider cannot insist that a particular contractor do the work. The housing provider may only require that whoever does the work is reasonably able to complete the work in a workmanlike manner and obtain all necessary building permits.

24. If a Person with a Disability has Made Reasonable Modifications to the Interior of the Dwelling, Must she Restore *all* of them when she Moves out?

The tenant is obligated to restore those portions of the interior of the dwelling to their previous condition only where "it is reasonable to do so" and where the housing provider has requested the restoration. The tenant is not responsible for expenses associated with reasonable wear and tear. In general, if the modifications do not affect the housing provider's or subsequent tenant's use or enjoyment of the premises, the tenant cannot be required to restore the modifications to their prior state. A housing provider may choose to keep the modifications in place at the end of the tenancy. See also Question 28.

Example 1: Because the tenant uses a wheelchair, she obtained permission from her housing provider to remove the base cabinets and lower the kitchen sink to provide for greater accessibility. It is reasonable for the housing provider to ask the tenant to replace the cabinets and raise the sink back to its original height.

Example 2: Because of a mobility disability, a tenant obtained approval from the housing provider to install grab bars in the bathroom. As part of the installation, the contractor had to construct reinforcements on the underside of the wall. These reinforcements are not visible and do not detract from the use of the apartment. It is reasonable for the housing provider to require the tenant to remove the grab bars, but it is not reasonable for the housing provider to require the tenant to remove the reinforcements.

Example 3: Because of a mobility disability, a tenant obtained approval from the housing provider to widen doorways to allow him to maneuver in his wheelchair. In usual circumstances, it is not reasonable for the housing provider to require him to restore the doorways to their prior width.

25. Of the Reasonable Modifications made to the Interior of a Dwelling that must be Restored, must the Person with a Disability Pay to Make those Restorations when she Moves out?

Yes. Reasonable restorations of the dwelling required as a result of modifications made to the interior of the dwelling must be paid for by the tenant unless the next occupant of the dwelling wants to retain the reasonable modifications and where it is reasonable to do so, the next occupant is willing to establish a new interest bearing escrow account. The subsequent tenant would have to restore the modifications to the prior condition at the end of his tenancy if it is reasonable to do so and if requested by the housing provider. See also Question 24.

26. If a Person with a Disability has Made a Reasonable Modification to the Exterior of the Dwelling, or a Common Area, Must she Restore it to its Original Condition when she Moves out?

No. The Fair Housing Act expressly provides that housing providers may only require restoration of modifications made to interiors of the dwelling at the end of the tenancy. Reasonable modifications such as ramps to the front door of the dwelling or modifications made to laundry rooms or building entrances are not required to be restored.

27. May a Housing Provider Increase or Require a Person with a Disability to Pay a Security Deposit if she Requests a Reasonable Modification?

No. The housing provider may not require an increased security deposit as the result of a request for a reasonable modification, nor may a housing provider require a tenant to pay a security deposit when one is not customarily required. However, a housing provider may be able to take other steps to ensure that money will be available to pay for restoration of the interior of the premises at the end of the tenancy. See Questions 21 and 28.

28. May a Housing Provider Take other Steps to Ensure that Money will be Available to Pay for Restoration of the Interior of the Premises at the End of the Tenancy?

Where it is necessary in order to ensure with reasonable certainty that funds will be available to pay for the restorations at the end of the tenancy, the housing provider may negotiate with the tenant as part of a restoration agreement a provision that requires the tenant to make payments into an interest-bearing escrow account. A housing provider may not routinely require that tenants place money in escrow accounts when a modification is sought. Both the amount and the terms of the escrow payment are subject to negotiation between the housing provider and the tenant.

Simply because an individual has a disability does not mean that she is less creditworthy than an individual without a disability. The decision to require that money be placed in an escrow account should be based on the following factors: 1) the extent and nature of the proposed modifications; 2) the expected duration of the lease; 3) the credit and tenancy history of the individual tenant; and 4) other information that may bear on the risk to the housing provider that the premises will not be restored.

If the housing provider decides to require payment into an escrow account, the amount of money to be placed in the account cannot exceed the cost of restoring the modifications, and the period of time during which the tenant makes payment into the escrow account must be reasonable. Although a housing provider may require that funds be placed in escrow, it does not automatically mean that the full amount of money needed to make the future restorations can be required to be paid at the time that the modifications are sought. In addition, it is important to note that interest from the account accrues to the benefit of the tenant. If an escrow account is established, and the housing provider later decides not to have the unit restored, then all funds in the account, including the interest, must be promptly returned to the tenant.

Example 1: Because of a mobility disability, a tenant requests a reasonable modification. The modification includes installation of grab bars in the bathroom. The tenant has an excellent credit history and has lived in the apartment for five years before becoming disabled. Under these circumstances, it may not be reasonable to require payment into an escrow account.

Example 2: Because of a mobility disability, a new tenant with a poor credit history wants to lower the kitchen cabinets to a more accessible height. It may be reasonable for the housing provider to require payment into an interest bearing escrow account to ensure that funds are available for restoration.

Example 3: A housing provider requires all tenants with disabilities to pay a set sum into an interest bearing escrow account before approving any request for a reasonable modification. The amount required by the housing provider has no relationship to the actual cost of the restoration. This type of requirement violates the Fair Housing Act.

29. What if a Person with a Disability Moves into a Rental Unit and Wants the Carpet Taken up because her Wheelchair does not Move Easily across Carpeting? Is that a Reasonable Accommodation or Modification?

Depending on the circumstances, removal of carpeting may be either a reasonable accommodation or a reasonable modification.

Example 1: If the housing provider has a practice of not permitting a tenant to change flooring in a unit and there is a smooth, finished floor underneath the carpeting, generally, allowing the tenant to remove the carpet would be a reasonable accommodation.

Example 2: If there is no finished flooring underneath the carpeting, generally, removing the carpeting and installing a finished floor would be a reasonable modification that would have to be done at the tenant's expense. If the finished floor installed by the tenant does not affect the housing provider's or subsequent tenant's use or enjoyment of the premises, the tenant would not have to restore the carpeting at the conclusion of the tenancy. See Questions 24 and 25.

Example 3: If the housing provider has a practice of replacing the carpeting before a new tenant moves in, and there is an existing smooth, finished floor underneath, then it would be a reasonable accommodation of his normal practice of installing new carpeting for the housing provider to just take up the old carpeting and wait until the tenant with a mobility disability moves out to put new carpeting down.

30. Who is Responsible for Paying for the Costs of Structural Changes to a Dwelling unit that has not yet been Constructed if a Purchaser with a Disability Needs Different or Additional Features to Make the Unit Meet her Disability-related Needs?

If the dwelling unit is not subject to the design and construction requirements (i.e., a detached single family home or a multi-story townhouse without an elevator), then the purchaser is responsible for the additional costs associated with the structural changes. The purchaser is responsible for any additional cost that the structural changes might create over and above what the original design would have cost.

If the unit being purchased is subject to the design and construction requirements of the Fair Housing Act, then all costs associated with incorporating the features required by the Act are borne by the builder. If a purchaser with a disability needs different or additional features added to a unit under construction or about to be constructed beyond those already required by the Act, and it would cost the builder more to provide the requested features, the structural changes would be considered a reasonable modification and the additional costs would have to be borne by the purchaser. The purchaser is responsible for any additional cost that the structural changes might create over and above what the original design would have cost.

Example 1: A buyer with a mobility disability is purchasing a single family dwelling under construction and asks for a bathroom sink with a floorless base cabinet with retractable doors that allows the buyer to position his wheelchair under the sink. If the cabinet costs more than the standard vanity cabinet provided by the builder, the buyer is responsible for the additional cost, not the full cost of the requested cabinet. If, however, the alternative cabinet requested by the buyer costs less than or the same as the one normally provided by the builder, and the installation costs are also the same or less, then the builder should install the requested cabinet without any additional cost to the buyer.

Example 2: A buyer with a mobility disability is purchasing a ground floor unit in a detached townhouse that is designed with a concrete step at the front door. The buyer requests that the builder grade the entrance to eliminate the need for the step. If the cost of providing the at-grade entrance is no greater than the cost of building the concrete step, then the builder would have to provide the at-grade entrance without additional charge to the purchaser.

Example 3: A buyer with a mobility disability is purchasing a unit that is subject to the design and construction requirements of the Fair Housing Act. The buyer wishes to have grab bars installed in the unit as a reasonable modification to the bathroom. The builder is responsible for installing and paying for the wall reinforcements for the grab bars because these reinforcements are required under the design and construction provisions of the Act. The buyer is responsible for the costs of installing and paying for the grab bars.

31. Are the Rules the Same if a Person with a Disability Lives in Housing that Receives Federal Financial Assistance and the Needed Structural Changes to the Unit or Common Area Are the Result of the Tenant Having a Disability?

Housing that receives federal financial assistance is covered by both the Fair Housing Act and Section 504 of the Rehabilitation Act of 1973. Under regulations implementing Section 504, structural changes needed by an applicant or resident with a disability in housing receiving federal financial assistance are considered reasonable accommodations. They must be paid for by the housing provider unless providing them would be an undue financial and administrative burden or a fundamental alteration of the program or unless the housing provider can accommodate the individual's needs through other means. Housing that receives federal financial assistance and that is provided by state or local entities may also be covered by Title II of the Americans with Disabilities Act.

Example 1: A tenant who uses a wheelchair and who lives in privately owned housing needs a roll-in shower in order to bathe independently. Under the Fair Housing Act the tenant would be responsible for the costs of installing the roll-in shower as a reasonable modification to his unit.

Example 2: A tenant who uses a wheelchair and who lives in housing that receives federal financial assistance needs a roll-in shower in order to bathe independently. Under Section 504 of the Rehabilitation Act of 1973, the housing provider would be obligated to pay for and install the roll-in shower as a reasonable accommodation to the tenant unless doing so was an undue financial and administrative burden or unless the housing provider could meet the tenant's disability-related needs by transferring the tenant to another appropriate unit that contains a roll-in shower.

HUD has provided more detailed information about Section 5 04's requirements. See www.hud.gov/offices/fheo/disabilities/sect504.cfm.

32. If a Person Believes that she has been Unlawfully Denied a Reasonable Modification, what should that Person Do if she Wants to Challenge that Denial under the Act?

When a person with a disability believes that she has been subjected to a discriminatory housing practice, including a provider's wrongful denial of a request for a reasonable modification, she may file a complaint with HUD within one year after the alleged denial or may file a lawsuit in federal district court within two years of the alleged denial. If a complaint is filed, HUD will investigate the complaint at no cost to the person with a disability.

There are several ways that a person may file a complaint with HUD:

- By placing a toll-free call to 1-800-669-9777 or TTY 1-800-927-9275;
- By completing the "on-line" complaint form available on the HUD internet site: http://www.hud.gov; or
- By mailing a completed complaint form or letter to:
  Office of Fair Housing and Equal Opportunity
  Department of Housing & Urban Development

451 Seventh Street, S.W., Room 5204
Washington, DC 204 10-2000

Upon request, HUD will provide printed materials in alternate formats (large print, audio tapes, or Braille) and provide complainants with assistance in reading and completing forms.

The Civil Rights Division of the Justice Department brings lawsuits in federal courts across the country to end discriminatory practices and to seek monetary and other relief for individuals whose rights under the Fair Housing Act have been violated. The Civil Rights Division initiates lawsuits when it has reason to believe that a person or entity is involved in a "pattern or practice" of discrimination or when there has been a denial of rights to a group of persons that raises an issue of general public importance. The Division also participates as *amicus curiae* in federal court cases that raise important legal questions involving the application and/or interpretation of the Act. To alert the Justice Department to matters involving a pattern or practice of discrimination, matters involving the denial of rights to groups of persons, or lawsuits raising issues that may be appropriate for *amicus* participation, contact:

U.S. Department of Justice
Civil Rights Division
Housing and Civil Enforcement Section – G St.
950 Pennsylvania Avenue, N.W.
Washington, DC 20530

For more information on the types of housing discrimination cases handled by the Civil Rights Division, please refer to the Housing and Civil Enforcement Section's website at http://www.usdoj.gov/crt/housing/hcehome.html.

A HUD or Department of Justice decision not to proceed with a Fair Housing Act matter does not foreclose private plaintiffs from pursuing a private lawsuit. However, litigation can be an expensive, time-consuming, and uncertain process for all parties. HUD and the Department of Justice encourage parties to Fair Housing Act disputes to explore all reasonable alternatives to litigation, including alternative dispute resolution procedures, such as mediation. HUD attempts to conciliate all Fair Housing Act complaints. In addition, it is the Department of Justice's policy to offer prospective defendants the opportunity to engage in pre-suit settlement negotiations, except in the most unusual circumstances.

ENDNOTES

[1] The Fair Housing Act is codified at 42 U.S.C. §§ 3601-3619.

[2] The Act uses the term "handicap" instead of "disability." Both terms have the same legal meaning. *See Bragdon v. Abbott,* 524 U.S. 624, 631 (1998) (noting that the definition of "disability" in the Americans with Disabilities Act is drawn almost verbatim "from the definition of 'handicap' contained in the Fair Housing Amendments Act of 1988"). This document uses the term "disability," which is more generally accepted.

[3] 42 U.S.C. § 3604(f)(3)(A).

[4] This Statement does not address the principles relating to reasonable accommodations. For further information see the Joint Statement of the Department of Housing and Urban Development and the Department of Justice: Reasonable Accommodations Under the Fair Housing Act, dated May 17, 2004. This Joint Statement is available at www.hud.gov/ offices/fheo/disabilities/index.cfm and http://www.usdoj.gov/crt/housing /jointstatement_ra.htm. See also 42 U. S.C. § 3 604(f)(3)(B). This Statement also does not discuss in depth the obligations of housing providers who are recipients of federal financial assistance to make and pay for structural changes to units and common and public areas that are needed as a reasonable accommodation for a person's disability. See Question 31.

[5] 42 U.S.C. § 3604(f)(3)(A). HUD regulations pertaining to reasonable modifications may be found at 24 C.F.R. § 100.203.

[6] The Act contemplates certain limits to the receipt of reasonable accommodations or reasonable modifications. For example, a tenant may be required to deposit money into an interest bearing account to ensure that funds are available to restore the interior of a dwelling to its previous state. *See, e.g.*, Question 21 below. A reasonable accommodation can be conditioned on meeting reasonable safety requirements, such as requiring persons who use motorized wheelchairs to operate them in a manner that

does not pose a risk to the safety of others or cause damage to other persons' property. *See* Joint Statement on Reasonable Accommodations, Question 11.

[7] Persons who meet the definition of disability for purposes of receiving Supplemental Security Income ("SSI") or Social Security Disability Income ("SSDI") benefits in most cases meet the definition of a disability under the Fair Housing Act, although the converse may not be true. *See, e.g., Cleveland v. Policy Management Systems Corp,* 526 U.S. 795, 797 (1999) (noting that SSDI provides benefits to a person with a disability so severe that she is unable to do her previous work and cannot engage in any other kind of substantial gainful work whereas a person pursuing an action for disability discrimination under the Americans with Disabilities Act may state a claim that "with a reasonable accommodation" she could perform the essential functions of the job).

[8] Housing providers that receive federal financial assistance are also subject to the requirements of Section 504 of the Rehabilitation Act of 1973. 29 U.S.C. § 794. Section 504, and its implementing regulations at 24 C.F.R. Part 8, prohibit discrimination based on disability, and obligate housing providers to make and pay for structural changes to facilities, if needed as a reasonable accommodation for applicants and tenants with disabilities, unless doing so poses an undue financial and administrative burden. See Question 31.

INDEX